BETWEEN THOUGHT AND EXPRESSION

BETWEEN THOUGHT AND EXPRESSION

SELECTED LYRICS OF

LOU REED

HYPERION NEW YORK

"The Calm Before the Storm," "Letters to the Vatican" © 1988 Metal Machine Music and Rubén Blades Productions, Inc.

"Small Town," "Nobody But You," "Hello It's Me," "A Dream," "It Wasn't Me" © 1990 Metal Machine Music and John Cale Music, Inc.

"The Slide," "Since Half the World is H_2O" originally appeared in *Unmuzzled Ox*, Vol. IV, No. 1, 1976.

"To Do the Right Thing": Lou Reed Interviews Václav Havel was first published in *Musician* magazine, October 1990.

Copyright © 1991, Metal Machine Music, Inc.

First Edition

Library of Congress Cataloging-in-Publication Data
Reed, Lou.
Between thought and expression : selected lyrics of Lou Reed.
p. cm.
Discography: p.
Includes index.
ISBN 1-56282-993-9 : $18.95
I. Title.
PS3568.E3673B48 1991
811'.54—dc20   91-22561
                                                          CIP

10 9 8 7 6 5 4 3 2 1

For
Sid, Toby, Bunny
And most of all
For Sylvia

CONTENTS

IN THE beginning was the word . . . closely followed by a drum and some early version of a guitar. This is a collection of lyrics that I feel can stand alone from the music for which they were originally written. I've also included two poems, one of which won an award from the Literary Council for Small Magazines, and two interviews—one with Václav Havel, the other with Hubert Selby. I did these pieces because they gave me the opportunity to meet two men I admired and find out more about writing—the how and why of it—which in the end revolves around life and how you live it.

Over the last few years I have done occasional "poetry" readings, always using my lyrics as the basis. I was continually struck by the different voices that emerged when the words were heard without music, and those experiences encouraged me to consider the possibility of publishing them naked.

The heart of a lyric for me has always been anchored in an experienced reality, whether it be Avedon's photo of Warhol's bullet-scarred chest or the sociopathic attitudes recorded in "Kicks" or "Street Hassle." So in answer to the question I am most often asked, "Are these incidents real?" Yes, he said, Yes Yes Yes.

—Lou Reed

THE LYRICS (1965-1990)

I'LL BE YOUR MIRROR

I'll be your mirror, reflect what you are
In case you don't know
I'll be the wind, the rain, and the sunset
The light on your door
To show that you're home

When you think the night has seen your mind
that inside you're twisted and unkind
Let me stand to show that you are blind
Please put down your hands
'cause I see you

I find it hard
to believe you don't know
The beauty you are
But if you don't,
let me be your eyes
A hand to your darkness
So you won't be afraid

When you think the night has seen your mind
that inside you're twisted and unkind
Let me stand to show that you are blind
Please put down your hands
'cause I see you

I'll be your mirror

I'M WAITING FOR THE MAN

I'm waiting for my man
Twenty-six dollars in my hand
Up to Lexington 1-2-5
Feeling sick and dirty more dead than alive
I'm waiting for my man

Hey white boy, what you doin' uptown
Hey white boy, you chasin' our women around
Oh pardon me sir, it's furthest from my mind
I'm just lookin' for a dear dear friend of mine
I'm waiting for my man

Here he comes, he's all dressed in black
PR* shoes and a big straw hat
He's never early, he's always late
First thing you learn is that you always gotta wait
I'm waiting for my man

Up to a brownstone, up three flights of stairs
Everybody's pinned you but nobody cares
He's got the works gives you sweet taste
Then you gotta split because he's got no time to waste
I'm waiting for my man

Baby don't you holler, darlin' don't you ball and shout
I'm feeling good, you know I'm gonna work it on out
I'm feeling good, I'm feeling oh so fine
Until tomorrow but that's just some other time
I'm waiting for my man

/ / *Puerto Rican Fence Climbers* / /

4

HEROIN

I don't know just where I'm going
But I'm going to try for the kingdom if I can
'Cause it makes me feel like I'm a man
When I put a spike into my vein
Then I tell you things aren't quite the same
When I'm rushing on my run
And I feel just like Jesus' son
And I guess that I just don't know
and I guess that I just don't know

I have made a big decision
I'm gonna try to nullify my life
'Cause when the blood begins to flow
When it shoots up the dropper's neck
When I'm closing in on death
You can't help me, not you guys
or all you girls with your sweet silly talk
You can all go take a walk
And I guess that I just don't know
and I guess that I just don't know

I wish that I was born a thousand years ago
I wish that I'd sailed the darkened seas
On a great big clipper ship
Going from this land here to that
Put on a sailor's suit and cap

/ / *I was one of the first Medicare patients. A drug I shot in San Francisco froze
all my joints. The doctors suspected terminal lupus but this turned out to
be untrue. Anyway, it didn't matter since I checked myself out of the hospital
to go to Delmore's funeral and never went back. I wrote the song in college.* / /

Away from the big city
Where a man cannot be free
Of all the evils of this town
And of himself and those around
And I guess that I just don't know
and I guess that I just don't know

Heroin, be the death of me
Heroin, it's my wife and it's my life
Because a mainer to my vein
Leads to a center in my head
And then I'm better off than dead
'Cause when the smack begins to flow
I really don't care anymore
About all you Jim-Jims in this town
And all the politicians making crazy sounds
And everybody putting everybody else down
And all the dead bodies piled up in mounds

'Cause when that heroin is in my blood
and that blood is in my head
Thank God I'm as good as dead
Thank your God that I'm not aware
and Thank God that I just don't care
And I guess that I just don't know
and I guess that I just don't know

BLACK ANGEL'S DEATH SONG

The myriad choices of his fate
set themselves out upon a plate
for him to choose what had he to lose
Not a ghost bloodied country all covered with sleep
where the black angel did weep
not an old city street in the east
gone to choose

And wandering's brother walked on through the night
with his hair
in his face
long a long splintered cut from a knife of G.T.

The Rally Man's patter ran on through the dawn
until we said so long to his skull
Shrill yell

Shining brightly, red rimmed and red lined with the time
effused with the choice of the mind on ice skates scraping chunks
from the bells

Cut mouths bleeding razors forget in the pain
antiseptic remains coo goodbye
so you fly
to the cozy brown snow of the east
Gone to choose, choose again

Sacrificial remain make it hard to forget
where you come from

/ / *The idea here was to string words together for the sheer fun of their sound, not any particular meaning. I loved the title.* / /

the stools of your eyes serve to realize pain
choose again

Roberman's refrain of the sacrilege recluse
for the loss of a horse
went the bowels in the tail of a rat
Come again, choose to go

And if epiphanies terror reduced you to shame
Have your head bobbed and weaved
Choose a side
to be on

If the stone glances off split didactics in two
Lay the colour of mouse trail's all's green try between
If you choose
If you choose
Try to lose
For the loss of remains come and start
start the game
I Chi Chi
Chi Chi I
Chi Chi Chi
Ka Ta Ko
Choose to choose
choose to lose
Choose to Go

VENUS IN FURS

Shiny, shiny, shiny boots of leather
Whiplash girlchild in the dark
Comes in bells your servant, don't forsake him
Strike dear mistress and cure his heart

Downy sins of streetlight fancies
Chase the costumes she shall wear
Ermine furs adorn imperious
Severin, Severin awaits you there

I am tired, I am weary
I could sleep for a thousand years
A thousand dreams that would awake me
Different colors made of tears

Kiss the boot of shiny shiny leather
Shiny leather in the dark
Tongue the thongs, the belt that does await you
Strike dear mistress and cure his heart

Severin, Severin, speak so slightly
Severin, down on your bended knees
Taste the whip, in love not given lightly
Taste the whip, now bleed for me

Shiny, shiny, shiny boots of leather
Whiplash girlchild in the dark
Severin, your servant, comes in bells, please don't forsake him
Strike, dear mistress and cure his heart

/ / *I wrote this after reading the book by Sacher-Masoch.* / /

ALL TOMORROW'S PARTIES

And what costume shall the poor girl wear
To all tomorrow's parties
A hand-me-down dress from who knows where
To all tomorrow's parties
And where will she go, and what shall she do
When midnight comes around
She'll turn once more to Sunday's clown
and cry behind the door

And what costume shall the poor girl wear
To all tomorrow's parties
Why silks and linens of yesterday's gowns
To all tomorrow's parties
And what will she do with Thursday's rags
When Monday comes around
She'll turn once more to Sunday's clown and cry behind the door

And what costume shall the poor girl wear
To all tomorrow's parties
For Thursday's child is Sunday's clown
For whom none will go mourning

A blackened shroud
A hand-me-down gown
Of rags and silks—a costume
Fit for one who sits and cries
For all tomorrow's parties

/ / *This was Andy's favorite song.* / /

LADY GODIVA'S OPERATION

Lady Godiva here dressed so demurely
Pats the head of another curly hair boy, just another toy
Sick with silence she weeps sincerely
saying words that have oh so clearly been said
so long ago

Draperies wrapped gently 'round her shoulder
Life has made her that much bolder now
that she's found out how

Dressed in silk, latin, lace and envy
Pride and joy of the latest penny faire
pretty passing care

Hair today now dipped in the water
Making love to every poor daughter's son
isn't it fun

Now today propping grace with envy
Lady Godiva peers to see if anyone's there
and hasn't a care

Doctor is coming the nurse thinks SWEETLY
turning on the machines that NEATLY pump air
the body lies bare
Shaved and hairless what once was SCREAMING
now lies silent and almost SLEEPING
the brain must have gone away

/ / *I had twenty-four shock treatments when I was seventeen years old. I suppose
it caused me to write things like this.* / /

Strapped securely to the white table
ether caused the body to wither and writhe
underneath the white light

Doctor arrives with knife and baggage
sees the growth as just so much cabbage
that now
must be cut away

Now comes the moment of Great! Great! Decision!
The doctor is making his first incision!
One goes here—one goes there

The ether tubes leaking says someone who's sloppy
Patient it seems is not so well sleeping
The screams echo up the hall
Don't panic someone give him pentathol instantly
Doctor removes his blade
cagily so from the brain
By my count of ten—
the head won't move

THE GIFT

Waldo Jeffers had reached his limit. It was now mid-August, which meant he had been separated from Marsha for more than two months. Two months, and all he had to show were three dog-eared letters and two very expensive long-distance phone calls. True, when school had ended and she'd returned to Wisconsin and he to Locust, Pennsylvania, she had sworn to maintain a certain fidelity. She would date occasionally, but merely as amusement. She would remain faithful.

But lately, Waldo had begun to worry. He had trouble sleeping at night, and when he did, he had horrible dreams. He lay awake at night, tossing and turning underneath his pleated quilt protector, tears welling in his eyes as he pictured Marsha, her sworn vows overcome by liquor and the smooth soothing of some Neanderthal, finally submitting to the final caresses of sexual oblivion. It was more than the human mind could bear.

Visions of Marsha's faithlessness haunted him. Daytime fantasies of sexual abandon permeated his thoughts, and the thing was, they wouldn't understand how she really was. He, Waldo, alone understood this. He had intuitively grasped every nook and cranny of her psyche. He had made her smile—she needed him, and he wasn't there. (Ahh. . . .)

The idea came to him on the Thursday before the Mummers' parade was scheduled to appear. He'd just finished mowing and edging the Edisons' lawn for a dollar fifty and then checked the mailbox to see

/ / *I wrote this my last year at Syracuse University, where I was an English major. John Cale of the Velvet Underground suggested we set it to music. We put the story on stereo left and the music stereo right so you could listen to one or the other or both.* / /

1 3

if there was at least a word from Marsha. There was nothing but a circular from the Amalgamated Aluminum Company of America inquiring into his awning needs. At least they cared enough to write. It was a New York company. You could go anywhere in the mails.

Then it struck him. He didn't have enough money to go to Wisconsin in the accepted fashion, true, but why not mail himself? It was absurdly simple. He would ship himself, parcel-post special delivery. The next day Waldo went to the supermarket to purchase the necessary equipment. He bought masking tape, a staple-gun, and a medium-sized cardboard box, just right for a person of his build. He judged that with a minimum of jostling, he could ride quite comfortably. A few airholes, some water, perhaps some midnight snacks, and it would probably be as good as going tourist.

By Friday afternoon, Waldo was set. He was thoroughly packed and the post office had agreed to pick him up at three o'clock. He had marked the package "fragile" and as he sat curled up inside, resting on the foam-rubber cushioning he'd thoughtfully included, he tried to picture the look of awe and happiness on Marsha's face, as she opened her door, saw the package, tipped the deliverer, and then opened it to see her Waldo finally there in person. She would kiss him, and then maybe they could see a movie. If he'd only thought of this before. Suddenly, rough hands gripped his package, and he found himself borne up. He landed with a thud in a truck and was off.

Marsha Bronson had just finished setting her hair. It had been a very rough weekend. She had to remember not to drink like that. Bill had been nice about it, though. After it was over, he'd said he still respected her, and after all it was certainly the way of nature, and even though, no, he did not love her, he did feel an affection for her.

And after all, they were grown adults. Oh, what Bill could teach Waldo. But that seemed many years ago.

Sheila Klein, her very very best friend walked in through the porch screen door and into the kitchen.

"Oh God, it's absolutely maudlin outside."

"I know what you mean, I feel all icky." Marsha tightened the belt on her cotton robe with the silk outer edge. Sheila ran her finger over some salt grains on the kitchen table, licked her fingers and made a face.

"I'm supposed to be taking these salt pills, but"—she wrinkled her nose—"they make me feel like throwing up."

Marsha started to pat herself under the chin, an exercise she had seen on television. "God, don't even talk about that." She got up from the table and went to the sink, where she picked up a bottle of pink and blue vitamins. "Want one? Supposed to be better than steak," and then attempted to touch her knees.

"I don't think I'll ever touch a daiquiri again." She gave up and sat down, this time nearer the small table that supported the telephone. "Maybe Bill will call," she said to Sheila's glance. Sheila nibbled on her cuticle.

"After last night, I thought maybe you'd be through with him."

"I know what you mean. My god, he was like an octopus—hands all over the place!" she gestured raising her arms upward in defense. "The thing is, after a while you get tired of fighting with him you know, and after all I didn't really do anything Friday and Saturday, so I kind of owed it to him—you know what I mean." She started to scratch.

Sheila was giggling with her hand over her mouth. "I tell you, I felt the same way and even, after a while," here she bent forward in a whisper, "I wanted to." Now she was laughing very loudly.

It was at this point that Mr. Jameson, of the Clarence Darrow Post Office, rang the doorbell of the large stucco-covered frame house. When Marsha Bronson opened the door, he helped her carry the package in. He had his yellow and his green slips of paper signed, and left with a fifteen cent tip that Marsha had gotten out of her mother's small beige pocketbook in the den.

"What do you think it is?" Sheila asked.

Marsha stood with her arms folded behind her back. She stared at the brown cardboard carton that sat in the middle of the living-room. "I don't know."

Inside the package, Waldo quivered with excitement as he listened to the muffled voices. Sheila ran her fingernail over the masking tape that ran down the center of the carton. "Why don't you look at the return address and see who it's from."

Waldo felt his heart beating. He could feel the vibrating footsteps. It would be soon.

Marsha walked around the carton and read the ink-scratched label. "God, It's from Waldo!"

"That schmuck," said Sheila.

Waldo trembled with expectation.

"Well you might as well open it," said Sheila, and both of them tried to lift the stapled flap.

"Oaah" said Marsha groaning, "he must have nailed it shut." They tugged on the flap again. "My god, you need a power drill to get this thing open." They pulled again. "You can't get a grip." They both stood still breathing heavily. "Why don't you get a scissor," said Sheila. Marsha ran into the kitchen, but all she could find was a little sewing scissor. Then she remembered that her father kept a collection of tools in the basement. She ran downstairs, and when she came back up, she had a large sheet-metal cutter in her hand. "This is the best I could find." She was very out of breath. "Here, you do it, I think I'm gonna die." She sank into her large fluffy couch and exhaled noisily. Sheila tried to make a slit between the masking tape and the end of the carboard flap, but the blade was too big and there wasn't enough room. "Goddamn this thing," she said feeling very exasperated. Then, smiling, "I got an idea." "What?" said Marsha. "Just watch," said Sheila, touching her finger to her head.

Inside the package, Waldo was so transfixed with excitement that he could barely breathe. His skin felt prickly from the heat and he could feel his heart beating in his throat. It would be soon.

Sheila stood quite upright and walked around to the other side of the package. Then she sank down to her knees, grasped the cutter by both handles, took a deep breath, and plunged the long blade through the middle of the package, through the masking tape, through the cardboard, through the cushioning, and right through the center of Waldo Jeffers' head, which split slightly and caused little rhythmic arcs of red to pulsate gently in the morning sun.

CHELSEA GIRLS

Here's Room 506
It's enough to make you sick
Bridget's all wrapped in foil
You wonder if she can uncoil
Here they come now
See them run now
Here they come now
Chelsea Girls

Here's Room 115
Filled with S & M queens
Magic marker row
You wonder just high they go
Here's Pope dear Ondine
Rona's treated him so mean
She wants another scene
She wants to be a human being

Pepper she's having fun
She thinks she's some man's son
Her perfect love's don't last
Her future died in someone's past
Here they come
See them run now
Here they come now
Chelsea Girls

Dear Ingrid's found her lick
She's turned another trick

/ / *This was written for the Warhol movie of the same name. Since it was*
written after the movie came out, it did not appear in it. / /

Her treats and times revolve
She's got problems to be solved

Poor Mary, she's uptight
She can't turn out her light
She rolled Susan in a ball
and now she can't see her at all

Dropout, she's in a fix
amphetamine has made her sick
white powder in the air
She's got no bones and can't be scared

Here comes Johnny Bore
He collapsed on the floor
They shot him up with milk
And when he died sold him for silk
Here they come now
See them run now
Here they come now
Chelsea Girls

SOME KINDA LOVE

Some kinds of love
Marguerita told Tom
Between thought and expression lies a lifetime
Situations arise because of the weather
and no kinds of love
are better than others

Some kinds of love
Marguerita told Tom
like a dirty French novel
the absurd courts the vulgar
and some kinds of love
the possibilities are endless
and for me to miss one
would seem to be groundless

I heard what you said
Marguerita heard Tom
And of course you're a bore
But at that you're not charmless
for a bore is a straight line
that finds a wealth in division
and some kinds of love
are mistaken for vision

Put jelly on your shoulder
Let us do what you fear most
That from which you recoil
but which still makes your eyes moist

Put jelly on your shoulder
lie down upon the carpet

between thought and expression
let us now kiss the culprit

I don't know just what it's all about
Put on your red pajamas and find out

CANDY SAYS

Candy says I've come to hate my body
and all that it requires in this world
Candy says I'd like to know completely
what others so discreetly talk about

Candy says I hate the quiet places
that cause the smallest taste of what will be
Candy says I hate the big decisions
that cause endless revisions in my mind

I'm gonna watch the blue birds fly over my shoulder
I'm gonna watch them pass me by
Maybe when I'm older
What do you think I'd see
If I could walk away from me

/ / *Candy was a drag queen. She would later die of cancer caused by hormone injections. Her real name was James Slattery. She came from Long Island.* / /

PALE BLUE EYES

Sometimes I feel so happy
Sometimes I feel so sad
Sometimes I feel so happy
But mostly you just make me mad
Baby you just make me mad
Linger on, your pale blue eyes
Linger on, your pale blue eyes

Thought of you as my mountain top
Thought of you as my peak
Thought of you as everything
I've had but couldn't keep
I've had but couldn't keep

If I could make the world as pure and strange as what I see
I'd put you in the mirror I put in front of me
I put in front of me

Skip a life completely, stuff it in a cup
She said money is like us in time
It lies but can't stand up
Down for you is up

It was good what we did yesterday
And I'd do it once again
The fact that you are married
Only proves you're my best friend
But it's truly, truly a sin
Linger on, your pale blue eyes
Linger on, your pale blue eyes

/ / *I wrote this for someone I missed very much. Her eyes were hazel. It's been recorded by a lot of people, but my favorite version is by Maureen Tucker.* / /

AFTERHOURS

If you close the door, the night could last forever
leave the sunshine out and say hello to never
All the people are dancing and they're having such fun
I wish it could happen to me
But if you close the door, I'd never have to see the day again

If you close the door, the night could last forever
Leave the wineglass out and drink a toast to never
Oh, someday I know someone will look into my eyes
and say hello—you're my very special one—
but if you close the door I'd never have to see the day again

Dark party bars
Shiny Cadillac cars
and the people on subways and trains
Looking gray in the rain
as they stand disarrayed
oh but people look well in the dark

And if you close the door the night could last forever
Leave the sunshine out and say hello to never
All the people are dancing and they're having such fun
I wish it could happen to me
'Cause if you close the door I'd never have to see the day again
I'd never have to see the day again

/ /   *I loved afterhours bars. It's where I first saw someone beaten to death. The*
woman I was with, Nico, threw a glass that shattered in a mob guy's face.
He thought the man in back of me did it.   / /

2 4

THE MURDER MYSTERY

A

candy screen wrappers of silkscreen fantastic, requiring memories, both lovely and guilt-free, lurid and lovely with twilight of ages, luscious and lovely and filthy with laughter, laconic giggles, ennui for the passions, in order to justify most spurious desires, rectify moments, most serious and urgent, to hail upon the face of most odious time, requiring replies most facile and vacuous, with words nearly singed, with the heartbeat of passions, spew forth with the grace of a tart going under, subject of great concern, noble origin

B

[denigrate obtuse and active verbs pronouns, skewer the sieve of the optical sewer, release the handle that holds all the gates up, puncture the eyeballs, that seep all the muck up, read all the books and the people worth reading and still see the muck on the sky of the ceiling]

/ / *This was another experiment. Lyric A was recorded on stereo left and at the same time lyric B was read on stereo right. The music was in the middle. I was having fun with words and wondering if you could cause two opposing emotions to occur at the same time. I'd fired John from the V.U.* / /

A

please   raise   the   flag
rosy   red   carpet   envy
english   used   here
this   messenger   is   nervous
it's   no   fun   at   all
out here in the hall

B

[mister   moonlight
succulent smooth and gorgeous
Isn't it nice? We're number one
and   so   forth
Isn't it sweet being unique?]

A

for screeching and yelling and
various offenses, lower the queen
and bend her over the tub, against
the state, the country, the
committee, hold her head under
the water please for an hour, for
groveling and spewing and
various offenses, puncture that
bloat with the wing of a sparrow,
the inverse, the obverse, the
converse, the reverse, the
sharpening wing of the edge of a
sparrow, for suitable reckonings
too numerous to mention, as the
queen is fat she is devoured by
rats, there is one way to skin a
cat or poison a rat it is hereto
four hear to three forthrightly
stated

put down that rag simpering,
callow   and   morose
who   let   you   in?
if I knew, then I could get out
the   murder   you   see
is   a   mystery   to   me

B

[relent and obverse and inverse
and perverse and reverse the
inverse of perverse and reverse
and reverse and reverse and
reverse and reverse and chop it
and pluck it and cut it and spit it
and sew it to joy on the edge of a
cyclop and spinet it to rage on
the edge of a cylindrical minute]

[dear   Mister   Muse
fellow of wit and gentry
medieval   ruse
filling   the   shallow   and
empty,   fools   that   duel
duel in pools]

A

to Rembrandt and Oswald, to
peanuts and ketchup,
sanctimonious sycophants stir
in the bushes, up to the stand
with your foot on the bible as
king I must order and constantly
arouse, if you swear to catch up
and throw up and up up, a king
full of virgin and kiss me and
spin it, excuse me to willow and
wander dark wonders, divest me
of robes-suture Harry and pig
meat, the fate of a nation, rests
hard on your bosoms, the king on
his throne, puts his hand down his
robe, the torture of inverse and
silk screen and Harry, and set
the tongue squealing the reverse
and inverse

B

[tantalize poets with visions of
grandeur, their faces turn blue
with the reek of the compost, as
the living try hard to retain
what the dead lost, with double
dead sickness from writing at
what cost and business and
business and reverse and reverse
and set the brain reeling the
inverse and perverse]

A					B			
objections			suffice		[English			arcane
apelike	and	tactile	bassoon		tantamount	here	to	frenzy
oboeing			me		passing	for		me
cordon	the	virus'	section		lascivious	elder		passion
off	to	the	left		corpulent			filth
is what is not right					disguised as silk			

A	**B**

A

contempt, contempt, and contempt
for the boredom, I shall poison
the city and sink it with fire, for
Cordless and Harry and Apepig
and Scissor, the messenger's wig
seems fraught with desire, for
blueberry picnics, and pince-nez
and magpies, the messenger's
skirt, would you please hook it
higher, for children and adults all
those under 90, how truly
disgusting! would you please put
it down? a stray in this fray is
no condom worth saving, as king
I'm quite just, but it's just quite
impossible, a robe and a robe
and a robe and a bat, no double class
inverse
could make lying worth dying

B

[with cheap simian melodies,
hillbilly outgush, for illiterate
ramblings for cheap
understandings, for mass
understanding the simple the
inverse, the compost, the
reverse, the obtuse and stupid,
and business, and business, and
cheap, stupid lyrics, and simple
mass reverse while the real thing
is dying]

A

accept the pig, enter the Owl
and Gorgeous, King on the left,
it on the right and primping
adjusting his nose as he reads
from his scroll

off with his head, take his head
from his neck off, requiring
memories both lovely and guilt-
free, put out his eyes, then cut
his nose off, sanctimonious
sycophants stir in the bushes,
scoop out his brain, put a string
where his ears were, all the
king's horses and all the king's
men, swing the whole mess at the
end of the wire, scratch out his
eyes with the tip of a razor, let
the wire extend from the tip of a
rose, Caroline, Caroline, Caroline,
Oh! but retain the remnants of
what once was a nose, pass me my
robe, fill my bath up with water

B

[folksy   knockwurst
peel back the skin of French and
what   do   you   find?   follicles
intertwining,   succulent   prose
wrapped up in robes]

[jumpsuit   and   pig   meat   and
making his fortune, while making
them happy with the inverse and
obverse and making them happy
and   making   them   happy
with the coy and the stupid,
just another dumb lackey, who
puts out the one thing, while
singing the other, but the real
thing's alone and it is no man's
brother]

	A					B				

A

B

no		one		knows		[safety		is		nice
no	nose	is	good	news	and	not	an	unwise	word	spoken
senseless						scary,		bad		dreams
extend		the		wine		made	safe	in	lovely	songs
drink	here	toast	to	selfless		no	doom		or	gloom
10	year	old		port		allowed in this room]				
is perfect in court										

A	**B**

Casbah and Cascade and Rosehip and Feeling, Cascade and Cyanide, Rachmaninoff, Beethoven-skull silly wagon and justice and perverse and reverse the inverse and inverse and inverse, blueberry catalog, questionable earnings, hustler's lament and the rest will in due cry, to battle and scramble and browbeat and hurt while chewing on minstrels and choking on dirt, disease please seems the order of the day, please the king, please the king, please the king day, Casbah and Cascade and Rosehip and Feeling, point of order return the king here to the ceiling

[oh, not to be whistled or studied or hummed or remembered at nights, when the I is alone, but to skewer and ravage and savage and split with the grace of a diamond, bellicose wit, to stun and to stagger with words as such stone, that those who do hear cannot again return home]

razzamatazz,
there's nothing on my shoulder, lust is a must, shaving my head's made me bolder, will you kindly read what it was I brought thee

[hello to Ray hello to Godiva and Angel who let you in? isn't it nice, the party? aren't the lights pretty at night?]

3 3

A

sick leaf and sorrow and pincers
net-scissors, regard and refrain
from the daughters of marriage,
regards for the elders and
youngest in carriage, regard and
regard for the inverse and
perverse and obverse, and
diverse, of reverse and reverse,
regard from the sick, the dumb,
and the camel from pump's storing
water, like brain is too marrow
to x-ray and filthy and cutting
and peeling to skin and to skin
and to bone and to structure to
livid and pallid and turgid and
structured and structured and
structured and structured and
structured and regard and refrain
and regard and refrain, the sick,
and the dumb, inverse, reverse
and perverse

B

[contempt, contempt, and
contempt for the seething, for
writhing and reeling and two-bit
reportage, for sick with the body
and sinister holy, the drowned
burst blue babies now dead on
the seashore, the valorous
horseman, who hang from the
ceiling, the pig on the carpet,
the dusty pale jissom, that has
no effect for the sick with the
see-saw, the inverse, obverse,
converse, reverse of reverse the
diverse and converse
of reverse and perverse
and sweet pyrotechnics, and
let's have another of inverse,
converse, diverse, perverse and
reverse, hell's graveyard is
damned as they chew on their
brains, the slick and the scum,
reverse, inverse and perverse]

A

plowing while it's done away
dumb and ready pig meat
sick upon the carpet
climb into the casket
safe within the parapet
sack is in the parapet
pigs are out and growling
slaughter by the seashore
see the lifeguard drowning
sea is full of fishes
fish's full of china
china plates are falling
all fall down
sick and shiny carpet
lie before my eyes eyes
lead me to the ceiling
walk upon the wall wall
tender as the green grass
drink the whisky horror
see the young girls dancing
flies upon the beaches
beaches are for sailors
nuns across the sea-wall
black hood horseman raging
swordsman eating fire

B

[sick upon the staircase
sick upon the carpet
blood upon the pillow
climb into the parapet
see the church bells gleaming
knife that scrapes a sick plate
dentures full of air holes
the tailor couldn't mend straight
shoot her full of air holes
climbing up the casket
take me to the casket
teeth upon her red throat
screw me in the daisies
rip apart her holler
snip the seas fantastic
treat her like a sailor
full and free and nervous
out to make his fortune
either this or that way
sickly or in good health
piss upon a building
like a dog in training
teach to heel or holler
yodel on a sing song
down upon the carpet]

A	B
fire on the carpet	[tickle polyester
set the house ablazing	sick within the parapet
seize and bring it flaming	screwing for a dollar
gently to the ground ground	sucking on a fire-hose
Dizzy Bell Miss Fortune	chewing on a rubber line
fat and full of love-juice	tied to chairs and rare bits
drip it on the carpet	pay another player
down below the fire hose	oh you're such a good lad
weep and whisky fortune	here's another dollar
sail me to the moon, dear	tie him to the bedpost
drunken dungeon sailors	sick with witches' covens
headless Roman horsemen	craving for a raw meat
the king and queen are empty	bones upon the metal
their heads are in the outhouse	sick upon the circle
fish upon the water	down upon the carpet
bowl upon the saviour	down below the parapet
toothless wigged Laureate	waiting for your bidding
plain and full of fancy	pig upon the carpet
name upon a letterhead	tumescent railroad
impressing all wheatgerm	neuro-anaesthesia analog
love you for a nickel	ready for a good look
ball you for a quarter	drooling at the birches
set the casket flaming	swinging from the birches
do not go gentle blazing	succulent Nebraska]

FERRYBOAT BILL

Ferryboat Bill, won't you please come home?
You know your wife has married a midget's son
And that's the short and long of it

THAT'S THE STORY OF MY LIFE

That's the story of my life
That's the difference between wrong and right
But Billy said, both those words are dead
That's the story of my life

/ / *The Factory photographer Billy Name told me this. He also told me I was*
a lesbian, so you have to take things with a grain of salt.   / /

ROCK 'N' ROLL

Jenny said when she was just five years old
There was nothing happenin' at all
Every time she puts on a radio
There was nothin' goin' down at all
Then one fine mornin' she puts on a New York station
She couldn't believe what she heard at all
She started dancin' to that fine fine music
You know her life was saved by rock 'n' roll
Despite all the amputations you could just
Dance to a rock 'n' roll station

Jenny said when she was just five years old
My parents are gonna be the death of us all
Two TV sets and two Cadillac cars—
Ain't gonna help me at all
Then one fine mornin' she puts on a New York station
She don't believe what she heard at all
She started dancin' to that fine fine music
You know her life was saved by rock 'n' roll
Despite all the computations
You could just dance to a rock 'n' roll station

And it was alright

SWEET JANE

Standin' on the corner
Suitcase in my hand
Jack is in his corset, Jane is in her vest
and me, I'm in a rock 'n' roll band
Ridin' in a Stutz Bear Cat, Jim
You know those were different times
All the poets they studied rules of verse
and those ladies they rolled their eyes

Jack he is a banker
and Jane, she is a clerk
and both of them save their monies
and when they come home from work
Sittin' down by the fire
The radio does play
The March of the Wooden Soldiers
and you can hear Jack say

Some people they like to go out dancin'
and other people they have to work
And there's even some evil mothers
Well there gonna tell you that everything is just dirt
You know that women never really faint
and that villains always blink their eyes
that children are the only ones who blush
and that life is just to die
But anyone who ever had a heart
They wouldn't turn around and break it
And anyone whoever played a part
They wouldn't turn around and hate it
Sweet Jane, Sweet Sweet Jane

N. Y. TELEPHONE CONVERSATION

I was sleeping gently napping when I heard the phone
Who is on the other end talking
Am I even home
Did you see what she did to him
Did you hear what they said
Just a New York conversation rattling in my head

Oh oh my, and what shall we wear
oh oh my, and who really cares

Just a New York conversation
Gossip all of the time
Did you hear who did what to whom
happens all the time
Who has touched and who has dabbled
here in the city of shows
Openings, closings, bad repartee
Everybody knows

Oh how sad, and why do we call
Oh I'm glad, to hear from you all

I am calling
Yes I'm calling
Just to speak to you
For I know this night will kill me
If I can't be with you
If-I-can't-be-with-you

WALK ON THE WILD SIDE

Holly came from Miami F-L-A
Hitchhiked her way across the U.S.A.
Plucked her eyebrows along the way
Shaved her legs and then he was a she
She says, Hey babe, take a walk on the wild side

Candy came from out on the Island
in the backroom she was everybody's darling
but she never lost her head even when she was giving head—
(the colored girls go
Doo do doo do doo)

Little Joe never once gave it away
Everybody had to pay and pay
A hustle here and a hustle there
New York City is the place where they say
Hey babe, take a walk on the wild side

The Sugar Plum Fairy came and he hit the streets
Lookin' for soul food and a place to eat
Went to the Apollo
You should've seen 'em go go go

Jackie is just speeding away
Thought she was James Dean for a day

/ / *They were going to make a musical out of Nelson Algren's* A Walk on the
Wild Side. *When they dropped the project I took my song and changed the
book's characters into people I knew from Warhol's Factory. I don't like to
waste things.* / /

Then I guess she had to crash
Valium would have helped that bash

Hey take a walk on the wild side
And the colored girls go doo do doo do doo

ANDY'S CHEST

If I could be anything in the world that flew
I would be a bat and come swooping after you
And if the last time you were here things were a bit askew
Well, you know what happens after dark
When rattlesnakes lose their skins and their hearts
And all the missionaries lose their bark
Oh, all the trees are calling after you
And all the venom snipers after you
Are all the mountains bolder after you?

If I could be anyone of the things in this world that bite
Instead of an ocelot on a leash, I'd rather be a kite
And be tied to the end of your string
and flying in the air, babe, at night
Cause you know what they say about honey bears
when you shave off all their baby hair
You have a hairy minded pink bare bear

And all the balls are rolling out for you
And stones are all erupting out for you
And all the cheap bloodsuckers are flying after you

Yesterday, Daisy Mae and Biff were grooving on the street
And just like in a movie her hands became her feet
Her belly button was her mouth
which meant she tasted what she'd speak

But the funny thing is what happened to her nose
It grew until it reached all of her toes
Now when people say her feet smell they mean her nose.

And curtains laced with diamonds dear for you
And all the Roman Noblemen for you

And kingdom's Christian Soldiers dear for you
And melting ice cap mountain tops for you
And knights in flaming silver robes for you
And bats that with a kiss turn prince for you
Swoop Swoop
oh baby, Rock Rock
Swoop Swoop
Rock Rock

MEN OF GOOD FORTUNE

Men of good fortune, often cause empires to fall
While men of poor beginnings, often can't do anything at all
The rich son waits for his father to die
The poor just drink and cry
And me, I just don't care at all

Men of good fortune, very often can't do a thing
While men of poor beginnings, often can do anything
At heart they try to act like a man
Handle things the best way they can
They have no rich daddy to fall back on

Men of good fortune, often cause empires to fall
while men of poor beginnings often can't do anything at all
It takes money to make money they say
Look at the Fords, didn't they start that way
Anyway, it makes no difference to me

Men of good fortune, often wish that they could die
While men of poor beginnings want what *they* have
And to get it they'll die
All those great things that life has to give
They want to have money and live
But me, I just don't care at all
about men of good fortune, men of poor beginnings

/ / *The following six songs were from an album called* Berlin. *It was a concept album in that the songs related to one another. You could think of it as boy gets girl boy loses girl. I'd never been to Berlin but I loved the idea of the then divided city.* / /

THE BED

This is the place where she lay her head
When she went to bed at night
And this is the place where our children were conceived
Candles lit the room at night

And this is the place where she cut her wrists
That odd and fateful night
And I said, oh, what a feeling

This is the place where we used to live
I paid for it with love and blood
And these are the boxes that she kept on the shelf
Filled with her poetry and stuff

And this is the room where she took the razor
And cut her wrists that strange and fateful night

I never would have started if I'd known
That it'd end this way
But funny thing I'm not at all sad
That it stopped this way

This is the place where she lay her head
when she went to bed at night
And this is the place our children were conceived
Candles lit the room brightly at night
And this is the place where she cut her wrists
That odd and fateful night
and I said, oh, oh, oh, oh, oh, oh, oh, what a feeling
I said oh—what a feeling

/ / *I'd gotten married.* / /

THE KIDS

They're taking her children away
Because they said she was not a good mother
They're taking her children away
Because she was making it with sisters and brothers
and everyone else, all of the others
Like cheap officers who would stand there and
Flirt in front of me

They're taking her children away
Because they said she was not a good mother
They're taking her children away
Because of the things that they heard she had done
The black Air Force sergeant was not the first one
And all of the drugs she took, every one, every one

And I am the Water Boy
the real game's not over here
But my heart is overflowing anyway
I'm just a tired man, no words to say . . .
But since she lost her daughter
It's her eyes that fill with water
and me, I am much happier this way

They're taking her children away
Because they said she was not a good mother

They're taking her children away
Because number one was the girlfriend from Paris
The things that they did they didn't have to ask us
And then the Welshman from India, who came here to stay

They're taking her children away
because they said she was not a good mother

They're taking her children away
Because of the things she did in the streets
In the alleys and bars, no she couldn't be beat
That miserable rotten slut couldn't turn anyone away

CAROLINE SAYS II

Caroline says, as she gets up off the floor
Why is it that you beat me, it isn't any fun
Caroline says, as she makes up her eye
You ought to learn more about yourself, think more than just I

She's not afraid to die
All of her friends call her Alaska
When she takes speed, they laugh and ask her
What-is-in-her-mind
What-is-in-your-mind

Caroline says—as she gets up from the floor
You can hit me all you want to, but I don't love you anymore
Caroline says, while biting her lip
Life is meant to be more than this—and this is a bum trip

She put her fist through the window pane
It was such a funny feeling

It's so cold in Alaska

SAD SONG

Staring at my picture book
She looks like Mary, Queen of Scots
She seemed very regal to me
Just goes to show you how wrong you can be
I'm gonna stop wasting my time
Somebody else would have broken both of her arms

My castle, kids and home
I thought she was Mary, Queen of Scots
I tried so very hard
Shows just how wrong you can be

I'm gonna stop wasting my time
Somebody else would have broken both of her arms

/ / *We got divorced.* / /

HOW DO YOU THINK IT FEELS

How do you think it feels
When you're speeding and lonely
How do you think it feels
When all you can say is if only
If only I had a little
If only I had some change
If only, if only, if only
How do you think it feels
and when do you think it stops

How do you think it feels
When you've been up for five days
Hunting around always, cause you're afraid of sleeping

How do you think it feels
To feel like a wolf and foxy
How do you think it feels
To always make love by proxy

How do you think it feels
And when do you think it stops!
When do you think it stops!

/ /   *By speed I mean injectable liquid Methedrine.*   / /

KICKS

Hey man, what's your style
How you get your kicks for livin'
Hey man, what's your style
How you get your adrenaline flowin' now now
When you cut that dude with that stiletto, man, you
You did it so, ah, crudely
When the blood come-a-down his chest
Don't you know it was a better than sex
now, now, now
It was-a-way-a better than gettin' laid—cause it's the
final thing to do,
Get somebody to, uh, come on to you
then you just
get somebody to now now come on to you and then
you kill them,
you kill them

'Cause I need kicks
Hey baby, I need some kicks, now
I'm gettin really bored, I need a need a need a some kicks

/ / *Some of my friends were criminals.* / /

KILL YOUR SONS

All your two bit psychiatrists are giving you electric shock
They said they'd let you live at home with mom and dad
Instead of mental hospitals
But every time you tried to read a book you couldn't
get to page seventeen
'cause you forgot where you were
So you couldn't even read

Mom informed me on the phone she didn't know what to do
about dad
He took an axe and broke the table aren't you glad you're
married
And sister she got married on Long Island
And her husband takes the train
He's big and he's fat—he doesn't have a brain

Creedmore treated me very good
but Payne Whitney was even better
And when I flipped out on PHC
I was so sad—I didn't even get a letter

All the drugs that we took, it really was a lot of fun
But when they shoot you up with thorazine on crystal smoke
You choke like a son of a gun

Don't you know?
They're gonna kill your sons

THE SLIDE

I've got nothing about gay guys
But, faggots, just like a cunt.
Years ago, wherever we would spot them,
Handles down, Alabama, small town
We'd take the ha, ha, so ha, I, he'd
Do the slide
Do the slide
Baby, you'd better slide.

Now they got their own baths, yay,
With entertainers, and shit
From the opera. Man.
Famous names, man,
Big ones.
But we know what they do
It's not the same thing.
It's guys like me, who, who, do, do, who
Hate them, beat them, Do, Do.
Want to beat them. Do.

They want to beat them
They want a young suck off
Show them that they wanna, Bang! go,
Take a *slide.*

Man, you better, you understand
What I'm saying, DECIDE

I only let a lady
Put a needle in my arm.

/ /   *This won the award. Senator Eugene McCarthy presented it to me. I wonder
if he read the poem. He was taller than he seemed on TV.*   / /

It's too intimate for cats.
Like sex with a rag on.

When she does it without a tie, hey,
She's one of the guys. Man.
She don't have to Slide. Who.
Except for the big ones. Do.

SINCE HALF THE WORLD IS H$_2$O

Having disregarded exhortations to join the
NAVY
We learn to swim.
Those who do not swim,
Learn to sail,
Or more bizarrely,
Water ski.
Others, who had not even conceived of water,
Oh they wish for dry land.
But as the continents are defined by the sea,
This is never wholly possible.

TEMPORARY THING

Hey now bitch, now baby you'd better
You'd better get outta here quick
Maybe you was getting, ah too rich
It ain't like we ain't never seen this thing before
And if it turns you around
then you'd better hit the door
But I know—it's just a temporary thing

You read too many books, you seen too many plays
and if things like this turn you away
Now look, hey look you'd better think about it twice
I know that your good breeding makes it seem—not so nice—but
uh huh, it's just a temporary thing

Where's the number, where's a dime and where's the phone
I feel like a stranger, I guess you're gonna go back home
Your mother, your father, your fucking brother
I guess they wouldn't agree with me
but I don't give two shits
they're no better than me
I know
it's just a temporary thing

VICIOUS CIRCLE

You're caught in a vicious circle
Surrounded by your so-called friend
You're caught in a vicious circle
and it looks like it will never end
Cause some people think that they like problems
and some people think that they don't
and for everybody who says yes
there's somebody whose starin' sayin' don't

You're caught in a vicious circle
surrounded by your so-called friend
you're caught in a vicious circle
and it looks like it will just never end
Cause some people think that it's nerves
and some people think that it's not
and some people think that it's the things that you do
and others think that you were cold when you were hot
They think that that's what it was all about

DIRT

It's been a long time since I've spoken to you
Was it the right time?
Your current troubles and you know they'll get much worse
I hope you know how much I enjoyed them
You're a pig of a person, there's a justice in this world
Hey, how about that?
Your lack of conscience and your lack of morality
Well, more and more people know all about it

We sat around the other night, me and the guys,
trying to find the right word
That would best fit and describe
you and people like you
That no principle has touched no principles baptized
How about that?
Who'd eat shit and say it tasted good
if there was some money in it for him
Hey, you remember that song by this guy from Texas whose name
was Bobby Fuller?
I'll sing it for you it went like this:
I fought the law and the law won—
I fought the law and the law won

You're just dirt

/ / *I was specifically referring to my manager-lawyer at the time.* / /

I WANNA BE BLACK

I wanna be black
Have natural rhythm
Shoot twenty feet of jism, too
and fuck up the Jews
I wanna be black
I wanna be a Panther
Have a girlfriend named Samantha
And have a stable of foxy whores
Oh I wanna be black
I don't wanna be a fucked up, middle class, college student
anymore
I just want to have a stable of foxy little whores
Yeah, yeah I wanna be black

I wanna be black
I wanna be like Martin Luther King
and get myself shot in spring
And lead a whole generation too
And fuck up the Jews

I wanna be black, I wanna be like Malcolm X
and cast a hex over President Kennedy's tomb
And have a big prick, too

I don't wanna be a fucked up, middle class, college student
anymore

I just wanna have a stable of foxy little whores
Yeah, yeah I wanna be black

/ / *Black is beautiful.* / /

STREET HASSLE
WALTZING MATILDA

PART I

Waltzing Matilda whipped out her wallet
the sexy boy smiled in dismay
She took out four twenties 'cause she liked round figures
Everybody's a queen for a day
Oh babe, I'm on fire and you know how I admire your body
why don't we slip away
Although I'm sure you're certain it's a rarity me flirtin'
sha-la-la-la this way
Oh sha-la-la-la-la, sha-la-la-la-la
Hey babe, come on let's slipaway

Luscious and gorgeous, oh what a hunk of muscle
call out the national guard
She creamed in her jeans as he picked up her means
from off of the formica topped bar
and cascading slowly, he lifted her wholly
and boldly out of this world
And despite people's derision she
proved to be more than a diversion and sha-la-la-la later on—
sha-la-la-la he entered her slowly and showed her where he was
coming from
and then sha-la-la-la he made love to her gently it was like
she'd never ever come
And then sha-la-la-la-la sha-la-la-la-la
when the sun rose and he made to leave
you know sha-la-la-la-la sha-la-la-la-la
neither one regretted a thing

STREET HASSLE
STREET HASSLE

PART II

Hey that cunt's not breathing, I think she's had too much
of something or other, you know what I mean?
I don't mean to scare you, but you're the one who came here and
you're the one who's got to take her when you leave
I'm not being smart or trying to be cold on my part and I'm not
gonna wear my heart on my sleeve
But you know, people get all emotional and sometimes, man
They don't act rational
They think they're on TV
Sha-la-la-la man—why don't you just slip away

You know I'm glad that we met man
It really was nice talking and I really wish that there was a
little more time to speak
But you know it could be a hassle trying to explain myself to a
police officer about how it was your old lady got herself stiffed
And it's not like we could help her, there was nothing no one
could do, and if there was man
you know I would have been the first
But when someone turns that blue, it's a universal truth
you just know that bitch will never fuck again
By the way, that's really some bad shit
that you came down to our place with
you ought to be more careful
around the little girls

It's either the best or it's the worst
and since I don't have to choose, I guess I won't
and I know this ain't no way to treat a guest
But why don't you grab your old lady by the feet

and just lay her out on the darkened street and by morning
she's just another hit-and-run

You know some people got no choice
they can't even find a voice
to talk with—
that they can call their own
So the first thing that they see
that allows them the right to be
why they follow it,
you know what that's called—

Bad Luck

CITY LIGHTS

Don't these city lights light these streets to life
Don't these crazy nights bring us together
Any rainy day, you can dance your blues away
Don't these city lights bring us together

Charlie Chaplin's cane, well it flicked away the rain
Things weren't quite the same, after he came here
But then when he left, upon our own request
Things weren't quite the same, after he left here

We're supposed to be
a land of liberty
and those city lights to blaze forever
But that little tramp, leaning on that street corner lamp
When he left us, his humor left us forever

Don't these city lights bring these streets to life
Don't these crazy nights bring us together
Any rainy day, you can dance your blues away
Don't these city lights bring us together

FAMILIES

Mama, you tell me how's the family
and mama, tell me how's things going by you
and little baby sister, I heard that you got married
and I heard that you had yourself a little baby girl, too
and here's some uncles and some cousins I know vaguely
and would you believe my old dog Chelsy's there, too
and would you believe nobody in this family wanted to keep her
and now that dog's more a part of this family than I am
and I don't come home much anymore
No I don't come home much anymore

and mama, I know how disappointed you are
and papa, I know that you feel the same way too
and no, I still haven't got married
and no, there's no grandson
planned here for you
and by the way daddy, tell me how's the business
I understand that your stock it's growing very high
no daddy, you're not a poor man anymore
and I hope you realize it
before you die

Please, come on let's not start this business again
I know how much you resent the life that I have

but one more time I don't want the family business
don't want to inherit it upon the day that you die
Really dad, you should have given it to my sister
you know, Elizabeth, you know Elizabeth
she has a better head for those things than I

/ /   *In real life I would never use the word Papa. Or Mom. Or Dad.*   / /

6 6

She lives practically around the corner
that's really the kind of child you could be proud of

But papa, I know this visit's a mistake
there's nothing here we have in common except our name
and families that live out in the suburbs
often make each other cry

and I don't think that I'll come home much anymore
No, no I don't think that I'll come home again

MY OLD MAN

When I was a young boy in Brooklyn going to public school
During recess in the concrete playground they lined us up by
twos
In alphabetical order, Reagan, Reed, and Russo
I still remember the names
And stickball and stoopball
Were the only games that we played
And I wanted to be like my old man
and I wanted to grow up to be like my old man
I wanted to dress like, I wanted to be just like
I wanted to act like my old man

And then like everyone else I started to grow
And I didn't want to be like my father anymore
I was sick of his bullying
And having to hide under a desk on the floor
And when he beat my mother, it made me so mad I could choke
And I didn't want to be like my old man
I didn't even want to look like my old man
I didn't even want to seem like my old man

A son watches his father, being cruel to his mother
And makes a vow to return only when
He is so much richer, in every way so much bigger
That the old man will never hit anyone again.

And can you believe what he said to me
He said, Lou, act like a man

/ / *I wrote this for my father.* / /

STANDING ON CEREMONY

Remember your manners
Will you please take your hat off
Your mother is dying
Listen to her cough

We were always standing on ceremony
We were always standing on ceremony

Can't you show some respect please
Although you didn't in real life
Your mother is dying
And I god damn well hope you're satisfied

We were always standing on ceremony
We were always standing on ceremony

So please play another song on that jukebox
Please play another pretty sad song for me
And if that phone rings
Tell them that you haven't seen me
If that phone rings
Tell them you haven't seen me for weeks

/ /   *And this for my mother.*   / /

LITTLE SISTER

You know it's hard for me
I can not use the phone
And in the shade of publicity no relationship is born
And I feel like a Hercules who's recently been shorn
but I have always loved my baby sister

Pick me up at eight
you'll see me on TV
I know I don't look well time's not been good to me
But please believe me
the blame is all on me
and I've always loved my baby sister

Remember when
we were younger when
you would wait for me at school
and teachers, friends and brazen sins
and I was often cruel
But you always believed in me
you thought I was the best
And now that I've got you alone let me get this off my chest

Pick a melody then count from one to ten
I'll make a rhyme up and then we'll try again
to laugh or cry, or give a sigh
to a past that might have been
and how much I really loved my baby sister

/ / *And this was for my sister.* / /

THINK IT OVER

Waking, he stared raptly at her face
On his lips, her smell, her taste
Black hair framing her perfect face
With her wonderful mind and her incredible grace
And so, he woke he woke her with a start
To offer her his heart
Once and for all, forever to keep
And the words that she first heard him speak
Were really very sweet
He was asking her to marry him, and to think it over
Baby think it over

She said somewhere there's a faraway place
where all is ordered and all is grace
No one there is ever disgraced
And everybody there is wise and everyone has taste
And then she sighed, well la-dee-dah-dee-dah
You and I have come quite far
And we really must watch what we say
because when you ask for someone's heart
You must know that you're smart
Smart enough to care for it
So I'm gonna think it over
Baby, I'm going to think it over

/ /   *I wrote this for my wife, Sylvia.*   / /

TEACH THE GIFTED CHILDREN

Teach the gifted children, teach them to have mercy
Teach them about sunsets, teach them about moonrise
Teach them about anger, the sin that comes with dawning
Teach them about flowers, the beauty of forgetfulness
Then take me to the river and put me in the water
Bless them and forgive them, Father cause they just don't know

All the gifted children, teach the gifted children
The ways of men and animals
Teach them about cities, the history of the mysteries
Their vices and their virtues
About branches that blow in the wind
Or the wages of their sins
Teach them of forgiveness, teach them about mercy
Teach them about music
and the cool and cleansing water
teach the gifted children
all the gifted children

/ / *I started out in the Brooklyn and Long Island public school systems and have hated all forms of school and authority ever since. That's one reason the Army wouldn't take me. I said I wanted a gun and would shoot anyone or anything in front of me. I was chewing on 750 milligram green placidyls at the time and competing with a drag queen and a junkie to get out. It was the one thing my shock treatments were good for.* / /

THE POWER OF POSITIVE DRINKING

Some like wine and some like hops
But what I really love is my scotch
It's the power of positive drinking
Some people ruin their drinks with ice
And then, they ask you for advice
They tell you, I've never told anyone this before.
They say, Candy is dandy but liquor makes quipsters
And I don't like mixers, or sippers or sob sisters
You know, you have to be real careful
where you sit down in a bar these days
And then some people drink to unleash their libidos
and other people drink to prop up their egos
It's my burden, man
people say I have the kind of face you can trust

Some people say alcohol makes you less lucid
And I think that's true if you're kind of stupid
I'm not the kind that gets himself burned twice
And some say liquor kills the cells in your head
And for that matter so does getting out of bed
When I exit, I'll go out gracefully, shot in my hand

/ /   *I tried to give up drugs by drinking.*   / /

UNDERNEATH THE BOTTLE

Oooh Wheee, look at me
Looking for some sympathy
It's the same old story—of man and his search for glory
And he found it, there underneath the bottles
Things are never good
Things go from bad to weird
Hey gimme another scotch with my beer
I'm sad to say I feel the same today—as I always do
gimme a drink to relax me
Oooh Wheee, liquor set me free
I can't do no work, with these shakes inside me
Awww fuck, I got the lousiest luck
I'm sick of this, underneath the bottle
Seven days make a week, on two of them I sleep
I can't remember what the hell I was doin'
I got bruises on my leg from I can't remember when
I fell down some stairs I was lyin' underneath the bottle
Ooooh Wheee
Son of a B
You get so down you can't get any lower
So long world you play too rough
and it's getting me all mixed up
I lost my pride and it's hidin'
There—
underneath the bottle

/ / *It didn't work.* / /

WAVES OF FEAR

Waves of fear attack in the night
Waves of revulsion—sickening sights
My heart's nearly bursting
My chest's choking tight
Waves of fear, waves of fear

Waves of fear
Squat on the floor
Looking for some pill, the liquor is gone
Blood drips from my nose, I can barely breathe
Waves of fear I'm too scared to leave

I'm too afraid to use the phone
I'm too afraid to put the light on
I'm so afraid I've lost control
I'm suffocating without a word
Crazy with sweat, spittle on my jaw
What's that funny noise,
what's that on the floor
Waves of fear
Pulsing with death
I curse at my tremors
I jump at my own step
I cringe at my terror
I hate my own smell
I know where I must be
I must be in hell

Waves of fear
Waves of fear

/ /   *I was now seeing a world-famous Dr. Feelgood who administered to various*
Heads of State. I wondered if they were in the same shape I was in.   / /

THE GUN

The man has a gun
He knows how to use it
Nine millimeter Browning, let's see what he can do
He'll point it at your mouth
Say that he'll blow your brains out
Don't you mess with me
I'm carrying a gun
Carrying a gun
Carrying a gun
Don't you mess with me
Carrying a gun
Get over there
Move slowly
I'll put a hole in your face
If you even breathe a word
Tell the lady to lie down
I want you to be sure to see this
I wouldn't want you to miss a second
Watch your wife
Carrying a gun
Shooting with a gun
Dirty animal

Carrying a gun
Carrying a gun
Watch your face
Carrying a gun
Carrying a gun
Carrying a gun
The animal dies with fear in his eyes

With a gun
Don't touch him
Stay away from him
He's got a gun

THE DAY JOHN KENNEDY DIED

I dreamed I was president of these United States
I dreamed I replaced ignorance, stupidity and hate
I dreamed the perfect union and the perfect law, undenied
And most of all I dreamed I forgot the day John Kennedy died

I dreamed that I could do the job that others hadn't done
I dreamed that I was uncorrupt and fair to everyone
I dreamed I wasn't gross or base, a criminal on the take
And most of all I dreamed I forgot the day John Kennedy died

I remember where I was that day I was upstate in a bar
The team from the university was playing football on T.V.
Then the screen went dead and the announcer said
"There's been a tragedy, there are unconfirmed reports the
President's been shot, and he may be dead or dying."
Talking stopped, someone shouted, "What?!"
I ran out to the street
People were gathered everywhere saying did you hear what they
said on TV
and then a guy in a Porsche with his radio on
hit his horn and told us the news
He said, "The president's dead, he was shot twice in the head
in Dallas, and they don't know by whom."

I dreamed that I was president of these United States
I dreamed that I was young and smart and it was not a waste
I dreamed that there was a point to life and to the human race
I dreamed I could somehow comprehend that someone
shot him in the face

/ / *My last year of college. I was drafted two weeks after graduation. As I said,*
they didn't take me. / /

THE HEROINE

The heroine stood up on the deck
The ship was out of control
The bow was being ripped to shreds
Men were fighting down below
The sea had pummeled them for so long
That they knew nothing but fear
And the baby's in his box, he thinks the door is locked
The sea is in a state, the baby learns to wait
For the heroine
Locked in his defense
He waits for the heroine

The mast was cracking as the waves were slapping
Sailors rolled across the deck
And when they thought no one was looking
They would cut a weaker man's neck
While the heroine dressed
In a virgin white dress
Tried to steer the mighty ship
But the raging storm wouldn't hear of it
They were in for a long trip

Baby's in a box, thinks the door is locked
He finds it hard to breathe, drawing in the sea

And where's the heroine
to fire off the gun
To calm the raging seas
and let herself be seized by
the baby in the box

/ /   *Jackie Kennedy trying to claw her way out of that car.*   / /

He thinks the door is locked
The woman has the keys
But there's no moment she can seize

The heroine
Who transcends all the men
Who are locked inside the box
Will she ever let him out—

The Heroine—
Strapped to the mast
The pale ascendant
Heroine

THE BLUE MASK

They tied his arms behind his back to teach him how to swim
They put blood in his coffee and milk in his gin
They stood over the soldier in the midst of the squalor
There was war in his body and it caused his brain to holler

Make the sacrifice
mutilate my face
If you need someone to kill
I'm a man without a will
Wash the razor in the rain
Let me luxuriate in pain
Please don't set me free
Death means a lot to me

The pain was lean and it made him scream he knew he was alive
They put a pin through the nipples on his chest
He thought he was a saint
I've made love to my mother, killed my father and my brother
What am I to do
When a sin goes too far, it's like a runaway car
It cannot be controlled
Spit upon his face and scream
There's no Oedipus today
This is no play you're thinking you are in
What will you say

Take the blue mask down from my face and look me in the eye
I get a thrill from punishment
I've always been that way
I loathe and despise repentance

/ / *Self-portrait.*   / /

You are permanently stained
Your weakness buys indifference
and indiscretion in the streets
Dirty's what you are and clean is what you're not
You deserve to be soundly beat

Make the sacrifice
Take it all the way
There's no "won't" high enough
To stop this desperate day
Don't take death away
Cut the finger at the joint
Cut the stallion at his mount
And stuff it in his mouth

AVERAGE GUY

I ain't no Christian or no born-again saint
I ain't no cowboy or a Marxist D.A.
I ain't no criminal or Reverend Cripple from the right
I am just your average guy, trying to do what's right
I'm just an average guy

An average guy—I'm just an average guy
I'm average looking and I'm average inside
I'm an average lover and I live in an average place
You wouldn't know me if you met me face to face
I'm just your average guy

I worry about money and taxes and such
I worry that my liver's big and it hurts to the touch
I worry about my health and bowels
And the crime waves in the street
I'm really just your average guy
Trying to stand on his own two feet
I'm just your average guy

Average looks
Average tastes
Average height
An average waist
Average in everything I do
My temperature is 98.2
I'm just your average guy
An average guy

/ / *So much for celebrity. Andy said, "You don't have to tell them the truth."*
And so sometimes I don't. / /

MY HOUSE

The image of the poet's in the breeze
Canadian geese are flying above the trees
A mist is hanging gently on the lake
My house is very beautiful at night
My friend and teacher occupies a spare room
He's dead—at peace at last the wandering Jew
Other friends had put stones on his grave
He was the first great man that I had ever met
Sylvia and I got out our Ouija Board
To dial a spirit—across the room it soared
We were happy and amazed at what we saw
Blazing stood the proud and regal name Delmore
Delmore, I missed all your funny ways
I missed your jokes and the brilliant things you said
My Dedalus to your Bloom, was such a perfect wit
And to find you in my house makes things perfect
I've really got a lucky life
My writing, my motorcycle, and my wife
And to top it all off a spirit of pure poetry
Is living in this stone and wood house with me
The image of the poet's in the breeze
Canadian geese are flying above the trees
A mist is hanging gently on the lake
Our house is very beautiful at night

/ /   *Delmore Schwartz was my teacher and friend. He was the smartest, funniest,
saddest person I'd ever met. He had a large scar on his forehead he said he
got dueling with Nietzsche. I was Dedalus to his Bloom. On a good day.*
     *Delmore was buried next to his mother, something he would have hated
almost as much as he hated his brother for having a vasectomy. Unless he
was lying. Or writing out loud.*   / /

LEGENDARY HEARTS

Legendary hearts, tearing us apart
with stories of their love
Their great transcendent loves
While we stand here and fight
And lose another night of legendary love

Legendary loves, haunt me in my sleep
Promises to keep, I never should have made
I can't live up to this
I'm good for just a kiss—not legendary love

Romeo oh Romeo, wherefore art thou Romeo
He's in a car or at a bar
or churning his blood with an impure drug
He's in the past and seemingly lost forever
He worked hard at being good
but his basic soul was stained not pure
And when he took his bow no audience was clapping

Legendary hearts, tear us all apart
Make our emotions bleed, crying out in need
No legendary love is coming from above
It's in this room right now

And you've got to fight to make what's right

MAKE UP MIND

I can't seem to make up my mind
I can't tell the colors that will fit this room
I can't tell a thing about you
Make up my mind
I can't seem to make up my mind
Are you laughing at me or telling a joke?
The cigarette on the sheet begins to smoke
Make up your mind
Right or left, up or down, in or out, straight or round
Love or lust, rain or shine
I can't seem to make up my poor mind

I can't seem to make up my mind
I can't tell the difference between wrong and right
Are you laughing at me in your sleep tonight?
Leaving me behind—

Why don't you make up your mind

BETRAYED

Betrayed—by the one who says she loves you
By the one who says she needs you
above all other men
Betrayed by her fragile, vicious beauty
Her father did his duty, and I lie down betrayed

Justice taught her competence—Her mother was like steel
Her cousins, they're all convicts
She alone rose above that wheel
But a motorcyclist no matter how good
Is slave to an oncoming truck
and the poison of her father, was her most pitiless luck

Three of us lie in this bed, night of infamy
One of us lies on our back, her father's in her head
And quick she turns, and slaps my face
And with her eyes open wide she screams
I hate you, I hate you, I hate you
But she's looking right past me

Betrayed—by the one who says she loves you
By the one who says she needs you above all other men
Betrayed by her fragile, vicious beauty
Her father did his duty
And I lie down betrayed

BOTTOMING OUT

I'm cruising fast on a motorcycle
down this winding country road
And I pass the gravel at the foot of the hill
Where last week I fell off
There's still some oil by this old elm tree
And a dead squirrel that I hit
But if you hadn't left, I would've struck you dead
So I took a ride instead

My doctor says she hopes I know, how lucky I can be
After all it wasn't my blood mixed in the dirt that night
But this violent rage, that turns inward
Can not be helped by drink
And we must really examine this
And I say I need another drink

I'm tearing down Rte. 80 East
the sun's on my right side
I'm drunk but my vision's good
And I think of my child bride
And on the left in shadows I see
something that makes me laugh
I aim that bike at that fat pothole beyond that underpass

/ /   *This is an AA term as well as a motorcycle expression. In both cases it means*
what it sounds like.   / /

HOME OF THE BRAVE

Here's to Johnny with his Jo and Micky's got a wife
And here's to Jerry he has got his Joyce
And me—I'm shaking
in my boots tonight
For the daughters and the sons lost in the home of the brave

Here's to Frank hit in some bar, in picturesque Brooklyn Heights
And here's to a friend who jumped in front of a train
At 7 o'clock one night
And another friend who thinks he lacks worth
has disappeared from sight
somewhere in the home of the brave

The stars are hiding in their clouds
The street lights are too bright
A man's kicking a woman who's clutching his leg tight
And I think suddenly of you and blink my eyes in fright
And rush off to the home of the brave

And everyday you have to die some
Cry some
Die some

/ / *My college roommate and friend, Lincoln, tried to commit suicide by jumping in front of a train. He lived but lost an arm and a leg. He then tried to become a stand-up comedian. Years later he was found starved to death in his locked apartment.* / /

THE LAST SHOT

The last shot should have killed me,
pour another drink
Let's drink to the last shot
And the blood on the dishes in the sink
Blood inside the coffee cup, blood on the table top
But when you quit, you quit
But you always wish
you knew it was your last shot
I shot blood at the fly on the wall
My heart almost stopped, hardly there at all
I broke the mirror with my fall, with my fall-fall-fall
Gimme a double, give yourself one, too
Gimme a short beer, one for you, too
And a toast to everything that doesn't move, that doesn't move
But when you quit, you quit
But you always wish you knew it was your last shot
But when you quit, you quit
But you always wish you knew it was your last shot
Whisky, bourbon, vodka, scotch
I don't care what it is you've got
I just want to know that it's my last shot, my last shot
I remember when I quit pretty good
See this here's where I chipped this tooth
I shot a vein in my neck and coughed up a Quaalude
On my last shot,
Here's a toast to all that's good and here's a toast to hate
And here's a toast to toasting and I'm not boasting
when I say I'm getting straight, when I say I'm getting straight

But when you quit, you quit
but you always wish you knew it was

your last shot
When you quit, you quit
But you always wish
you knew it was your last shot

NEW SENSATIONS

I don't like guilt be it stoned or stupid
Drunk or disorderly I ain't no cupid
Two years ago today I was arrested on Christmas Eve
I don't want pain, I want to walk not be carried
I don't want to give it up, I want to stay married
I ain't no dog tied to a parked car

I want the principles of a timeless muse
I want to eradicate my negative views
And get rid of those people who are always on a down
It's easy enough to tell what is wrong
But that's not what I want to hear all night long
Some people are like human Tuinals

I took my GPZ out for a ride
The engine felt good between my thighs
The air felt cool it was forty degrees outside
I rode to Pennsylvania near the Delaware Gap
Sometimes I got lost and had to check the map
I stopped at a roadside diner for a burger and a Coke
There were some country folk and some hunters inside
Somebody got themselves married and somebody they died
I went to the jukebox and played a hillbilly song
They was arguing about football, as I waved and went outside
And I headed for the mountains, feeling warm inside
I love that GPZ so much you know that I could kiss her

/ / *I got busted in Riverhead for trying to cash someone else's illegal script. I
spent Christmas in the dangerous tier when it was discovered that someone
with my name who was wanted for murder had escaped from jail in upstate
New York. It turned out he was black. Or so they said. Cop humor.*
    I was defended by one of Richard Nixon's Watergate lawyers. / /

DOIN' THE THINGS THAT
WE WANT TO

The other night we went to see Sam's play
(Doin' the things that we want to)
It was very physical it held you to the stage
(Doin' the things that we want to)
The guy's a cowboy from some rodeo
(Doin' the things that he wants to)
The girl had once loved him but now she wants to go
Doin' the things she wants to
Doin' the things that she wants to
The man was bullish, the woman was a tease
(Doin' the things that they want to)
They fought with their words, their bodies and their deeds
(Doin' the things that we want to)
And when they finished fighting, they exited the stage
(Doin' the things that we want to)
And I was firmly struck by the way they had behaved
Doin' the things that they want to
Doin' the things that they want to

It reminds me of the movies Marty made about New York
Those frank and brutal movies that are so brilliant
Fool for Love meet The Raging Bull
They're very inspirational I love the things they do
Doin' the things that they want to
Doin' the things that they want to

There's not much you hear on the radio today
But you can still see a movie or a play—

/ / *This was written after seeing Sam Shepard's play* Fool for Love. *The other*
characters are from Marty Scorsese's Mean Streets.   / /

Here's to Travis Bickle and Here's to Johnny Boy
Growing up on the mean streets of New York

I wrote this song 'cause I'd like to shake your hand
(Doin' the things that we want to)
In a way you guys are the best friends I ever had

FLY INTO THE SUN

I would not run from the holocaust
I would not run from the bomb
I'd welcome the chance to meet my maker
And fly into the sun
Fly into the sun
Fly into the sun
I'd break up into a million pieces and fly into the sun

I would not run from the blazing light
I would not run from its rain
I'd see it as an end to misery as an end to worldly pain
An end to worldly pain—An end to worldly pain
I'd shine by the light of the unknown moment
To end this worldly pain

The earth is weeping, the sky is shaking
The stars split to their core
And every proton and unnamed neutron is fusing in my bones
And an unnamed mammal is darkly rising
As man burns from his tomb
And I look at this as a blissful moment to fly into the sun
Fly into the sun—Fly into the sun
I'd burn up into a million pieces and fly into the sun
To end this mystery, answer my mystery
I'd look at this as a wondrous moment to end this mystery
Fly into the sun—Fly into the sun
I'd break up into a million pieces and fly into the sun

MY FRIEND GEORGE

Read in the paper about a man killed with a sword
And that made me think of my friend George
People said the man was five foot six
Sounds like Georgie with his killing stick

I knew Georgie since he's eight
I always thought that he was great
Anything that George would do
you know that I would do it too
George liked music and George liked to fight
He worked out in a downtown gym every night
I'd spar with him when work was done
We split lips but it was all in fun
Hey bro, what's the word
Talkin' bout my friend George

Next thing I hear George's got this stick
And using it for more than kicks
I seen him down at Smalley's bar
He was wired up I tried to calm him down
Avenge yourself he says to me—Avenge yourself for humanity
Avenge yourself for the weak and the poor
Stick it to these guys right through their heads
The fight is my music, the stick is my sword
And you know that I love you, so please don't say a word
Can't you hear the music playing, the anthem, it's my call
And the last I seen of Georgie was him running through the door

I says hey bro, what's the word—Talkin' bout my friend George
I says hey bro, what's the word—You talkin' bout my friend
George?!

MAMA'S GOT A LOVER

Mama's Got a Lover
A painter I am told
She's getting out of real estate
For the art scene down in old SoHo

Mama's Got a Lover
He owns a gallery
She says he likes collages but
The money's in GRA-FI-TI

Mama's Got a Lover
I met him yesterday
She says she hopes I like him
Maybe I'll send him a card on Father's Day

Mama's Got a Lover
They're backing a film
It's about a working mother
Who gives birth to black and white
Siamese twins

Mama's Got a Lover
He's got something to say
He says he's into dirt and rot
The essence of "urban decay"

Mama's Got a Lover
We met yesterday
She says she hopes I like him
I'll send him a card on Father's Day

Mama's Got a Lover
I met him yesterday
She's starting a new chapter
I wish she was on the last page

VIDEO VIOLENCE

The currents rage deep inside us
This is the age of video violence
The currents rage deep down inside us
This is the age of video violence

Up in the morning, drinking his coffee
Turns on the TV to some slasher movie
Cartoon-like women, tied up and sweaty
Panting and screaming
Thank you, have a nice day

His heart is pounding he switches the channel
looking for something other than rape or murder
or beatings or torture
but except for Walt Disney
it's a twisted alliance
This age of video violence

Down at his job his boss sits there screaming
If he loses his job, life loses its meaning
His son is in high school
There's nothing he's learning
He sits by the TV
Watching Corvettes exploding

The currents rage deep inside us
This is the age of video violence
The currents rage deep inside us
This is the age of video violence
Down at a bar some woman is topless
She's acned and scarred, her hair is a mess
While he shoves $5 down her exotic panties

The video jukebox is playing Madonna
While just down the block
At some local theater
they're grabbing their crotches
at the 13th beheading
As the dead rise to live
The live sink to die
The currents are deep and raging inside

Our good working stiff looks a whore in the eye
ties her to a bed
while he beats her back bloody
and then back at home
drinking more instant coffee
calls some red-neck evangelist
He's seen on TV and says

The currents rage, the dawn's upon us
This is the age of video violence
No age of reason is landing upon us
This is the age of video violence

The currents rage so deep within us
This is the age of video violence
The currents rage so deep down inside us
This is the age of video violence

THE ORIGINAL WRAPPER

I was sittin' home on the West End
Watchin' cable TV with a female friend
We were watchin' the news, the world's in a mess
the poor and the hungry, a world in distress
herpes, AIDS, the Middle East at full throttle
better check that sausage before you put it in the waffle
and while you're at it—check what's in the batter
Make sure that candy's in the
Original Wrapper

Reagan says abortion's murder
While he's looking at Cardinal O'Connor
Look at Jerry Falwell, Louis Farrakhan
both talk religion and the brotherhood of man
they both sound like they belong in Teheran
Watch out, they're goin' full throttle
better check that sausage before you stick it in the waffle
and while you're at it better check what's in the batter
Make sure that candy's in the
Original Wrapper
Hey, pitcher, better check that batter
Make sure that candy's in the
Original Wrapper

White against white, Black against Jew
It seems like it's 1942
the baby sits in front of MTV watching violent fantasies
while Dad guzzles beer with his favorite sport
only to find his heroes are all coked up
it's classic, original—the same old story
the politics of hate in a new surrounding
hate if it's good and hate if it's bad
and if this all don't make you mad

I'll keep yours and I'll keep mine
Nothing sacred and nothing divine
Father, bless me—We're at full throttle
better check that sausage before you put it in the waffle
and while you're at it better check that batter
Make sure the candy's in the Original Wrapper

I was born in the United States
I grew up hard but I grew up straight
I saw a lack of morals and a lack of concern
a feeling that there's nowhere to turn
Yippies, Hippies and upwardly mobile Yuppies
don't treat me like I'm some dumb lackey
Cause the murderer lives while the victims die,
I'd much rather see it an eye for an eye
A heart for a heart, a brain for a brain
and if this all makes you feel a little insane
kick up your heels—turn the music up loud
pick up your guitar and look out at the crowd
and say, "Don't mean to come on sanctimonious
but life's got me nervous and a little pugnacious—
lugubrious so I give a salutation
and rock on out to beat really stupid
ohh poop ah doo and how do you do
hip hop gonna bop till I drop."
Watch out world, comin' at you full throttle
better check that sausage before you put it in the waffle
and while you're at it better check that batter
Make sure the candy's in the Original Wrapper
Hey pitcher better check that batter
Make sure the candy's in the
Original Wrapper

TELL IT TO YOUR HEART

I'm staring through a telescope at night
at a large light in the sky
Its spinning lights reminded me of you
A star spinning in orbit lighting up the sky
or maybe it was not a star at all

I was standing by the Hudson River's edge at night
looking out across the Jersey shore
at a neon light spelling out some cola's name
And I thought
Your name should be dancing, beamed from satellites
Larger than any billboard in Times Square

Tell it to your heart
Please don't be afraid
I'm the one who loves you in each and every way
Tell it to your heart
Please don't be afraid
New York City lovers
Tell it to your heart

I'm up on the roof, it's 5 a.m. I guess I couldn't sleep
and I see this spinning light that I saw last week
Maybe I should wake you but by then it may be gone
You never know what you see if you look up in the sky

I ran outside down a darkened street listening
to my boot heels click
My leather jacket squeaked I needed a cigarette
When I turned the corner my spinning light was in the street
They were filming a commercial on TV

Tell it to your heart
Please don't be afraid
We're no teenage movie
That ends in tragedy
Tell it to your heart
Please don't be afraid
New York City lovers
Tell it to your heart

LETTERS TO THE VATICAN

Rosie sits inside a bar smoking a large man's cigar
In a place called "Sammy's" on Amsterdam Avenue
She doesn't look a day over 65, although she's really 29
She likes records from the '60s
They remind her of the good old times

And after some wine and some scotch
Rosie starts to let it hang out:
She throws a glass at the mirror and asks Big Max for a pen

She writes a letter to the Vatican
"I'm gonna write a letter to Him:
Dear Pope, send me some soap and a bottle of Bombay gin"
A letter to the Vatican
"I'm gonna write a letter to Him:
Dear Pope, send some hope or a rope to do me in"

And no one stops her
We all lend a hand
We all knew her before she was this mad
We just hold her until the shaking stops
Because the heart says what only the heart knows

"I wanna hear some Diana Ross
I wanna hear a little bit of Marvin Gaye
I wanna hear a song that reminds me of a better day"

Rosie slaps a pretty girl in the mouth
and running to the jukebox she tries to put a quarter in

/ / *I wrote these songs with Rubén Blades for his first English-lyric album,*
Nothing But the Truth. / /

She says, "I've had enough of you men
and I'll never say yes again; it's holiness or nothing
for me in this life . . ."

She writes a letter to the Vatican
"I'm gonna write a letter to him:
Dear Pope, send me some soap and a bottle of Bombay gin"
A letter to the Vatican
"I'm gonna write a letter to him:
Dear Pope, send me some hope or a rope to do me in"

And no one stops her
We all lend a hand
We all knew her before she was this mad
We just hold her until the shaking stops
Because the heart says what only the heart knows

THE CALM BEFORE THE STORM

There was a time when ignorance made our innocence strong
There was a time when we all thought we could do no wrong
There was a time, so long ago
but here we are in the calm before the storm

While the orchestra plays
they build barricades to help close the doors
While the musician sings
the holocaust rings the cymbals of war
We stare
at the things that were there
and no longer are—
And in our hearts
here we are again
In the calm before the storm

There was a time when we had an idea whose time hadn't come
They kept changing its name so we could still pretend
it was not really gone
We heard our screams turn into songs and back into screams again
And here we are again,
In the calm before the storm

ROMEO HAD JULIETTE

Caught between the twisted stars the plotted lines the faulty map
that brought Columbus to New York
Betwixt between the east and west
he calls on her wearing a leather vest
the earth squeals and shudders to a halt
A diamond crucifix in his ear is used to help ward off the fear
that he has left his soul in someone's rented car
Inside his pants he hides a mop
to clean the mess that he has dropped
into the life of lithesome Juliette Bell

And Romeo wanted Juliette
and Juliette wanted Romeo

Romeo Rodriguez squares his shoulders and curses Jesus
runs a comb through his black pony-tail
He's thinking of his lonely room
The sink that by his bed gives off a stink
then smells her perfume in his eyes
and her voice was like a bell

Outside the streets were steaming the crack dealers were dreaming
of an Uzi someone had just scored
I betcha I could hit that light
with my one good arm behind my back
says little Joey Diaz

/ / *The summer I wrote the New York album all the beaches were being closed
due to medical wastes washing up on shore. There was the Howard Beach
incident, the riots in Tompkins Square Park—in other words the
usual.* / /

Brother, give me another tote
those downtown hoods are no damn good
Those Italians need a lesson to be taught

This cop who died in Harlem you think they'd get the warnin'
I was dancing when his brains ran out on the street

and Romeo had Juliette
and Juliette had her Romeo

I'll take Manhattan in a garbage bag
with Latin writ on it that says
"It's hard to give a shit these days"*
Manhattan's sinking like a rock, into the filthy Hudson
what a shock
They wrote a book about it, they said it was like Ancient Rome
The perfume burned his eyes, holding tightly to her thighs
and something flickered for a minute
and then it vanished and was gone

*ASPERVM AESTIMARE FIMI ALIQVID HODIE

THE HALLOWEEN PARADE

There's a downtown fairy singing out "Proud Mary"
as she cruises Christopher Street
And some southern queen is acting loud and mean
where the docks and the badlands meet
This Halloween is something to be sure
Especially to be here without you

There's a Greta Garbo and an Alfred Hitchcock
and some black Jamaican stud
There's five Cinderellas and some leather drags
I almost fell into my mug
There's a Crawford, Davis and a tacky Cary Grant
and some homeboys lookin' for trouble down here from the Bronx

But there ain't no Hairy and no Virgin Mary
you won't hear those voices again
And Johnny Rio and Rotten Rita
you'll never see those faces again
This Halloween is something to be sure
Especially to be here without you

There's the Born Again Losers and the Lavender Boozers
and some crack team from Washington Heights
The boys from Avenue B, the girls from Avenue D
A Tinkerbell in tights
This celebration somehow gets me down
Especially when I see you're not around

/ / *This song was about the annual Halloween Parade in the Village and how
AIDS had vanquished so many of the participants.* / /

There's no Peter Pedantic saying things romantic
in Latin, Greek or Spic
There's no three bananas or Brandy Alexander
dishing all their tricks
It's a different feeling that I have today
Especially when I know you've gone away

There's a girl from SoHo with a tee-shirt saying "I blow"
She's with the "Jive Five 2 Plus 3"
and the girls for pay dates are giving cut rates
or else doing it for free
The past keeps knock knock knocking on my door
and I don't want to hear it anymore

No consolations please
for feelin' funky
I got to get my head above my knees
But it makes me mad and mad makes me sad
and then I start to freeze
In the back of my mind I was afraid it might be true
In the back of my mind I was afraid that they meant you
The Halloween Parade
see you next year—
at the Halloween Parade

DIRTY BLVD.

Pedro lives out of the Wilshire Hotel
he looks out a window without glass
The walls are made of cardboard
newspapers on his feet
and his father beats him 'cause he's too tired to beg
He's got 9 brothers and sisters
They're brought up on their knees
It's hard to run when a coat hanger beats you on the thighs
Pedro dreams of being older and killing the old man
But that's a slim chance he's going to The Boulevard

This room cost 2,000 dollars a month
You can believe it man it's true
Somewhere a landlord's laughing till he wets his pants
No one here dreams of being a doctor or a lawyer or anything
They dream of dealing on The Dirty Boulevard

Give me your hungry, your tired, your poor I'll piss on 'em
that's what the Statue of Bigotry says
Your poor huddled masses—let's club 'em to death
and get it over with and just dump 'em on The Boulevard

Outside it's a bright night, there's an opera at Lincoln Center
movie stars arrive by limousine
The klieg lights shoot up over the skyline of Manhattan
but the lights are out on the mean streets

A small kid stands by the Lincoln Tunnel
He's selling plastic roses for a buck
The traffic's backed up to 39th street
The TV whores are calling the cops out for a suck

And back at the Wilshire, Pedro sits there dreaming
He's found a book on magic in a garbage can
He looks at the pictures and stares up at the cracked ceiling
"At the count of 3," he says, "I hope I can disappear
and fly fly away . . ."

ENDLESS CYCLE

The bias of the father runs on through the son
leaving him bothered and bewildered
The drugs in his veins only cause him to spit
at the face staring back in the mirror
How can he tell a good act from the bad
He can't even remember his name
How can he do what needs to be done
When he's a follower and not a leader
The sickness of the mother runs on through the girl
leaving her small and helpless
Liquor flies through her brain with the force of a gun
leaving her running in circles
How can she tell a good act from the bad
when she's flat on her back in her room
How can she do what needs to be done
when she's a coward and a bleeder
The man if he marries will batter his child
and have endless excuses
The woman sadly will do much the same
thinking that it's right and it's proper
Better than their mommy or their daddy did
better than the childhood they suffered
The truth is they're happier when they're in pain
In fact, that's why they got married

BEGINNING OF A GREAT ADVENTURE

It might be fun to have a kid that I could kick around
A little me to fill up with my thoughts
A little me or he or she to fill up with my dreams
A way of saying life is not a loss
I'd keep the tyke away from school
and tutor him myself
Keep him from the poison of the crowd
But then again pristine isolation
might not be the best idea
It's not good trying to immortalize yourself

Why stop at one, I might have ten, a regular TV brood
I'd breed a little liberal army in the woods
Just like these redneck lunatics I see at the local bar
With their tribe of mutant inbred piglets with cloven hooves
I'd teach 'em how to plant a bomb, start a fire, play guitar
and if they catch a hunter, shoot him in the nuts
I'd try to be as progressive as I could possibly be
as long as I don't have to try too much

Susie, Jesus, Bogart, Sam, Leslie, Jill and Jeff
Rita, Winny, Andy, Fran and Jet
Boris, Bono, Lucy, Ethel, Bunny, Reg and Tom
that's a lot of names to try not to forget
Carrie, Marlon, Mo and Steve
La Rue and Jerry Lee
Eggplant, Rufus, Dummy, Star and The Glob
I'd need a damn computer to keep track of all these names
I hope this baby thing don't go too far

I hope it's true what my wife said to me
she says, baby, "It's the beginning of a great adventure"

It might be fun to have a kid that I could kick around
Create in my own image like a god
I'd raise my own pallbearers to carry me to my grave
and keep me company when I'm a wizened toothless clod
Some gibbering old fool sitting all alone drooling on his shirt
Some senile old fart playing in the dirt
It might be fun to have a kid I could pass something on to
Something better than rage, pain, anger and hurt

LAST GREAT AMERICAN WHALE

They say he didn't have an enemy
His was a greatness to behold
He was the last surviving progeny
The last one on this side of the world
He measured half a mile from tip to tail
silver and black with powerful fins
They say he could split a mountain in two
that's how we got the Grand Canyon

Some say they saw him at the Great Lakes
Some say they saw him off the coast of Florida
My mother said she saw him in Chinatown
but you can't always trust your mother
Off the Carolinas the sun shines brightly in the day
The lighthouse glows ghostly there at night
The chief of a local tribe had killed a racist mayor's son
and he'd been on death row since 1958
The mayor's kid was a rowdy pig
Spit on Indians and lots worse
The Old Chief buried a hatchet in his head
Life compared to death for him seemed worse
The tribal brothers gathered in the lighthouse to sing
and tried to conjure up a storm or rain

The harbor parted and the great whale sprang full up
and caused a huge tidal wave
The wave crushed the jail and freed the chief
The tribe let out a roar
The whites were drowned
The browns and reds set free
but sadly one thing more
Some local yokel member of the NRA

kept a bazooka in his living room
and thinking he had the Chief in his sights
blew the whale's brains out with a lead harpoon

Well Americans don't care for much of anything
Land and water the least
And animal life is low on the totem pole
with human life not worth more than infected yeast
Americans don't care too much for beauty
They'll shit in a river, dump battery acid in a stream
They'll watch dead rats wash up on the beach
and complain if they can't swim
They say things are done for the majority
Don't believe half of what you see
and none of what you hear

It's a lot like what my painter friend Donald said to me,
"Stick a fork in their ass and turn 'em over, they're done"

BUSLOAD OF FAITH

You can't depend on your family
You can't depend on your friends
You can't depend on a beginning
You can't depend on an end
You can't depend on intelligence
You can't depend on God
You can only depend on one thing
You need a busload of faith to get by

You can depend on the worst always happening
You can depend on a murderer's drive
You can bet that if he rapes somebody
There'll be no problem having a child
And you can bet that if she aborts it
Pro-lifers will attack her with rage
You can depend on the worst always happening
You need a busload of faith to get by

You can't depend on the goodly hearted
The goodly hearted made lampshades and soap
You can't depend on the Sacrament
No Father, no Holy Ghost
You can't depend on any churches
Unless there's real estate you want to buy
You can't depend on a lot of things
You need a busload of faith to get by

You can't depend on no miracle
You can't depend on the air
You can't depend on a wise man
You can't find them because they're not there

You can depend on cruelty
Crudity of thought and sound
You can depend on the worst always happening
You need a busload of faith to get by

HOLD ON

There's blacks with knives and whites with clubs
fighting at Howard Beach
There's no such thing as human rights
when you walk the N.Y. streets
A cop was shot in the head by a 10 year old kid named Buddah
in Central Park last week
The fathers and daughters are lined up by
the coffins by the Statue of Bigotry

You better hold on something's happening here
You better hold on—well I'll meet you in Tompkins Square

The dopers sent a message to the cops last weekend
they shot him in the car where he sat
and Eleanor Bumpers and Michael Stewart must have appreciated that
There's a rampaging rage rising up like a plague of bloody vials
washing up on the beach
It'll take more than the angels or Iron Mike Tyson
to heal this bloody breach

A junkie ran down a lady a pregnant dancer
she'll never dance but the baby was saved
He shot up some china white and nodded out at the wheel
and he doesn't remember a thing
They shot that old lady 'cause they thought she was a witness
to a crime she didn't even see

Whose home is the home of the brave by the statue of bigotry

/ / The New York Times *reprinted this on their Op-Ed page under the title*
"Anarchy in the Streets." / /

You got a black .38 and a gravity knife
You still have to ride the train
There's the smelly essence of N.Y. down there
but you ain't no Bernard Goetz
There's no mafia lawyer to fight in your corner
for that 15 minutes of fame
The have and the have nots are bleeding in the tub
That's New York's future not mine

GOOD EVENING MR. WALDHEIM

Good Evening, Mr. Waldheim
and Pontiff, how are you?
You have so much in common in the things you do
and here comes Jesse Jackson
He talks of common ground
Does that common ground include me
or is it just a sound
A sound that shakes
Oh Jesse, you must watch the sounds you make
A sound that quakes
There are fears that still reverberate

Jesse you say common ground
Does that include the PLO?
What about people right here right now
who fought for you not so long ago?
The words that flow so freely
falling dancing from your lips
I hope that you don't cheapen them with a racist slip
Oh common ground
Is common ground a word or just a sound
Common ground—remember those civil rights workers buried in
   the ground

If I ran for president and once was a member of The Klan
wouldn't you call me on it
The way I call you on Farrakhan
and Pontiff, pretty Pontiff
Can anyone shake your hand?
Or is it just that you like uniforms and someone kissing your hand

/ /   *Anti-Semitism, like patriotism, is the last refuge of a scoundrel.*   / /

Or is it true
The common ground for me includes you, too

Good Evening, Mr. Waldheim
Pontiff, how are you
As you both stroll through the woods at night
I'm thinking thoughts of you
and Jesse you're inside my thoughts
as the rhythmic words subside
My common ground invites you in
or do you prefer to wait outside
Or is it true
The common ground for me is without you
Or is it true
There's no ground common enough for me and you

XMAS IN FEBRUARY

Sam was lyin' in the jungle
agent orange spread against the sky like marmalade
Hendrix played on some foreign jukebox
They were praying to be saved
Those gooks were fierce and fearless
That's the price you pay when you invade
Xmas in February

Sam lost his arm in some border town
His fingers are mixed with someone's crop
If he didn't have that opium to smoke
the pain would never ever stop
Half his friends are stuffed into black body bags
with their names printed at the top
Xmas in February

Sammy was a short order cook in a
short order black and blue collar town
Everybody worked the steel mill but
the steel mill got closed down
He thought if he joined the army
he'd have a future that was sound
Like no Xmas in February

Sam's staring at the Vietnam Wall
It's been a while now that he's home
His wife and kid have left, he's unemployed

/ / *A legless Vietnam vet with AIDS (his cardboard sign read) strapped to a
skateboard begging outside H & H Bagels—the same spot where the night
before a law student was kicked in the throat and killed by a drunk from
a local bar who said the student insulted his boots.* / /

He's a reminder of the war that wasn't won
He's the guy on the street with the sign that reads
"Please help send this vet home"
But he is home
and there's no Xmas in February
No matter how much he saves

STRAWMAN

We who have so much
To you who have so little
To you who don't have anything at all
We who have so much
More than any one man does need
And you who don't have anything at all
Does anybody need another million dollar movie
Does anybody need another million dollar star
Does anybody need to be told over and over
Spitting in the wind comes back at you twice as hard

Strawman, going straight to the devil
Strawman, going straight to hell

Does anyone really need a billion dollar rocket
Does anyone need a $60,000 car
Does anyone need another president
or the sins of Swaggart parts 6,7,8 and 9
Does anyone need another politician
Caught with his pants down
Money sticking in his hole
Does anyone need another racist preacher
Spittin' in the wind can only do you harm

Does anyone need another faulty shuttle
Blasting off to the moon, Venus or Mars
Does anyone need another self-righteous rock singer
Whose nose he says led him straight to God
Does anyone need yet another blank skyscraper
if you're like me I'm sure a minor miracle will do
A flaming sword or maybe a gold ark floating up the Hudson
When you spit in the wind it comes right back at you

SICK OF YOU

I was up in the morning with the TV blarin'
Brushed my teeth sittin' watchin' the news
All the beaches were closed the ocean was a red sea
but there was no one there to part it in two
There was no fresh salad 'cause
there's hypos in the cabbage
Staten Island disappeared at noon
And they say the Midwest is in great distress
and NASA blew up the moon
The ozone layer has no ozone anymore
and you're gonna leave me for the guy next door
I'm sick of you
They arrested the mayor for an illegal favor
sold the Empire State to Japan
and Oliver North married Richard Secord
and gave birth to a little Teheran
And the Ayatollah bought a nuclear warship
if he dies he wants to go out in style
And there's nothing to eat that don't carry the stink
of some human waste dumped in the Nile
Well one thing is certainly true
No one here knows what to do
I'm sick of you
The radio said there were 400 dead
in some small town in Arkansas
Some whacked out trucker drove into a nuclear reactor
and killed everybody he saw
Now he's on Morton Downey
and he's glowing and shining
Doctors say this is a medical advance

/ / *This was a fantasy newscast.* / /

They say the bad makes the good
and there's something to be learned
in every human experience
Well I know one thing that really is true
This here's a zoo and the keeper ain't you
and I'm sick of it, I'm sick of you
They ordained the Trumps and then he got the mumps
and died being treated at Mount Sinai
And my best friend Bill died from a poison pill
some wired doctor prescribed for stress
My arms and legs are shrunk
the food all has lumps
They discovered some animal no one's ever seen
It was an inside trader eating a rubber tire
After running over Rudy Giuliani
They say the president's dead
no one can find his head
It's been missing now for weeks
but no one noticed it
He had seemed so fit
and I'm sick of it
I'm sick of you

THERE IS NO TIME

This is no time for celebration
This is no time for shaking hands
This is no time for back slapping
This is no time for marching bands
This is no time for optimism
This is no time for endless thought
This is no time for my country right or wrong
Remember what that brought

There is no time

This is no time for congratulations
This is no time to turn your back
This is no time for circumlocution
This is no time for learned speech
This is no time to count your blessings
This is no time for private gain
This is a time to put up or shut up
It won't come back this way again

There is no time

This is no time to swallow anger
This is no time to ignore hate
This is no time to be acting frivolous
because the time is getting late

This is no time for private vendettas
This is no time to not know who you are
Self-knowledge is a dangerous thing
The freedom of who you are
This is no time to ignore warnings

This is no time to clear the plate
Let's not be sorry after the fact
and let the past become our fate

There is no time

This is no time to turn away and drink
or smoke some vials of crack
This is a time to gather force
and take dead aim and attack
This is no time for celebration
This is no time for saluting flags
This is no time for inner searchings
The future is at hand
This is no time for phony rhetoric
This is no time for political speech
This is a time for action
because the future's within reach

This is the time, because there is no time

DIME STORE MYSTERY

He was lying banged and battered, skewered
and bleeding, talking crippled on the cross
Was his mind reeling and heaving
hallucinating fleeing what a loss
The things he hadn't touched or kissed
his senses slowly stripped away
Not like Buddha not like Vishnu
Life wouldn't rise through him again
I find it easy to believe
that he might question his beliefs
The beginning of the Last Temptation
Dime Store Mystery

The duality of nature, godly nature, human nature
Splits the soul
Fully human, fully divine and divided
The great immortal soul
Split into pieces, whirling pieces, opposites attract
From the front, the side, the back
The mind itself attacks
I know this feeling, I know it from before
Descartes through Hegel
Belief is never sure
Dime Store Mystery, Last Temptation

I was sitting drumming, thinking, thumping, pondering
The mysteries of life

/ / *At the Mass at St. Patrick's I realized I really wouldn't see Andy again.*
Somehow I'd expected him to be there, surrounded by his latest entourage,
smiling, saying, "Oh, hi. Where have you been? Why haven't you been
around?" It was my second funeral. My second wake. / /

Outside the city shrieking screaming whispering
The mysteries of life
There's a funeral tomorrow at St. Patrick's
The bells will ring for you
What must you have been thinking
when you realized the time had come for you
I wish I hadn't thrown away my time
on so much human and so much less divine
The end of the Last Temptation
the end of a Dime Store Mystery

SMALL TOWN

When you're growing up in a small town
When you're growing up in a small town
When you're growing up in a small town
You say no one famous ever came from here
When you're growing up in a small town
And you're having a nervous breakdown
And you think that you'll never escape it
Yourself or the place that you live
Where did Picasso come from
There's no Michelangelo coming from Pittsburgh
If art is the tip of the iceberg
I'm the part sinking below
When you're growing up in a small town
Bad skin, bad eyes—gay and fatty
People look at you funny
When you're in a small town
My father worked in construction
It's not something for which I am suited
Oh—what is something for which you are suited?
Getting out of here
I hate being odd in a small town
If they stare let them stare in New York City
At this pink eyed painting albino
How far can my fantasy go?
I'm no Dali coming from Pittsburgh
No adorable lisping Capote
My hero—oh do you think I could meet him?

The following is a selection of 5 songs that I wrote with John Cale delineat-
ing Andy Warhol's life on an album entitled Songs for 'Drella. *It was*
written for the stage and first performed at St. Ann's Church in Brooklyn,
my home town. / /

I'd camp out at his front door

There's only one good thing about a small town
There's only one good use for a small town
There's only one good thing about a small town
You know that you want to get out

When you're growing up in a small town
You know you'll grow down in a small town
There's only one good use for a small town
You hate it and you know you'll have to leave

NOBODY BUT YOU

I really care a lot although I look like I do not
since I was shot there's nobody but you
I know I look blasé, party Andy's what the papers say
at dinner I'm the one who pays—for a nobody like you
nobody but you, a nobody like you
since I got shot there's nobody but you

Won't you decorate my house
I'll sit there quiet as a mouse
you know me I like to look a lot—at nobody like you
I'll hold your hand and slap my face
I'll tickle you to your disgrace
Won't you put me in my proper place—a nobody like you

Sundays I pray a lot, I'd like to wind you up
and paint your clock
I want to be what I am not—for a nobody like you
The bullet split my spleen and lung, the doctors said I was gone
Inside I've got some shattered bone for nobody but you

I'm still not sure I didn't die
and if I'm dreaming I still have bad pains inside
I know I'll never be a bride—to nobody like you
I wish I had a stronger chin, my skin was good, my nose was thin
This is no movie I'd ask to be in—with a nobody like you
nobody like you, a nobody like you, all my life—
it's been nobodies like you

/ / *I sat in an ice cream shop late one night watching Andy take the hand of
a less than ordinary person sitting opposite him and slap his (Andy's) own
face with it. It somehow reminded me of Delmore raging in a bar, asking
me to call the White House to tell them we were aware of the plot.* / /

IT WASN'T ME

It wasn't me who shamed you, it's not fair to say that
You wanted to work I gave you a chance at that
It wasn't me who hurt you, that's more credit than I'm worth
Don't threaten me with the things you'll do to you

It wasn't me who shamed you, it wasn't me who brought
you down
You did it to yourself without any help from me
It wasn't me who hurt you, I showed you possibilities
The problems you had were there before you met me

I didn't say this had to be
You can't blame these things on me
It wasn't me, it wasn't me, it wasn't me,
I know she's dead, it wasn't me

It wasn't me who changed you, you did it to yourself
I'm not an excuse for the hole that you dropped in
I'm not simpleminded but I'm no father to you all
Death exists but you do things to yourself

I never said give up control
I never said stick a needle in your arm and die
It wasn't me, it wasn't me, it wasn't me
I know he's dead but it wasn't me

It wasn't me who shamed you, who covered you with mud
You did it to yourself without any help from me

/ / *Andy did some incredibly generous things for me. But he had made it clear*
he was not some mutant artist-father responsible for all of us. This often
resulted in cruelty, but I agreed with his position. / /

You act as if I could've told you or stopped you like some god
But people never listen and you know that that's a fact

I never said slit your wrists and die
I never said throw your life away
It wasn't me, it wasn't me, it wasn't me
You're killing yourself—you can't blame me

HELLO IT'S ME

Andy it's me, haven't seen you in a while
I wished I talked to you more when you were alive
I thought you were self-assured when you acted shy
Hello it's me
I really miss you, I really miss your mind
I haven't heard ideas like that for such a long, long time
I loved to watch you draw and watch you paint
But when I saw you last I turned away

When Billy Name was sick and locked up in his room
You asked me for some speed, I thought it was for you
I'm sorry if I doubted your good heart
Things always seem to end before they start

Hello it's me, that was a great gallery show
Your cow wallpaper and your floating silver pillows
I wish I paid more attention when they laughed at you
Hello it's me

"Pop goes pop artist," the headline said
"Is shooting a put-on, is Warhol really dead?"
You get less time for stealing a car
I remember thinking as I heard my own record in a bar

They really hated you, now all that's changed
But I have some resentments that can never be unmade
You hit me where it hurt I didn't laugh
Your Diaries are not a worthy epitaph

/ / *My wife and I were in a car with Andy. It was snowing out and the driver
was speeding. I asked him to slow down. Andy turned to me and in a fey,
arch whiny voice said, "You wouldn't have said that a few years ago." He
was being evil so I never spoke to him again.* / /

Oh well now Andy—I guess we've got to go
I wish someway somehow you like this little show
I know this is late in coming but it's the only way I know
Hello it's me—goodnight Andy . . .

A DREAM

I HAD a terrible dream the other night. Billy Name and Brigid were playing under my staircase on the second floor about two 'o clock in the morning. I woke up because Amos and Archie had started barking. That made me very angry because I wasn't feeling well and I told them. I was very cross the real me, that they just better remember what happened to Sam the Bad Cat that was left at home and got sick and went to pussy heaven.

It was a very cold clear fall night. Some snowflakes were falling, gee it was so beautiful, and so I went to get my camera to take some pictures. And then I was taking the pictures but the exposure thing wasn't right and I was going to call Fred or Gerry to find out how to get it set but oh it was late and then I remembered they were still probably at dinner and anyway I felt really bad and didn't want to talk to anybody anyway but the snowflakes were so beautiful and real looking and I really wanted to hold them. And that's when I heard the voices from down the hall near the stairs. So I got a flashlight and I was scared and I went out into the hallway. There's been all kinds of trouble lately in the neighborhood and someone's got to bring home the bacon and anyway there were Brigid and Billy playing. And under the staircase was a little meadow sort of like the park at 23rd street where all the young kids go and play frisbee, gee that must be fun, maybe we should do an article on that in the magazine, but they'll just tell me I'm stupid and it won't sell, but I'll just hold my ground this time, I mean it's my magazine isn't it?

So I was thinking that as the snowflakes fell and I heard those voices having so much fun. Gee it would be so great to have some fun. So I called Billy, but either he didn't hear me or he didn't want to answer which was so strange because even if I don't like reunions I've always loved Billy. I'm so glad he's working. I mean it's different

/ / *This is not an excerpt from Warhol's diaries. I wrote this trying to capture the love of the Andy I knew both inside and out.* / /

than Ondine. He keeps touring with those movies and he doesn't even pay us and the film, I mean the film's just going to disintegrate and then what. I mean he's so normal off of drugs. I just don't get it.

And then I saw John Cale. And he's been looking really great. He's been coming by the office to exercise with me. Ronnie said I have a muscle but he's been really mean since he went to AA. I mean what does it mean when you give up drinking and then you're still so mean. He says I'm being lazy but I'm not, I just can't find any ideas. I mean I'm just not, let's face it, going to get any ideas up at the office.

And seeing John made me think of the Velvets and I had been thinking about them when I was on St. Marks Place going to that new gallery those sweet new kids have opened, but they thought I was old, and then I saw the old Dom, the old club where we did our first shows. It was so great. And I don't understand about that Velvet's first album. I mean I did the cover and I was the producer and I always see it repackaged and I've never gotten a penny from it. How could that be. I should call Henry, but it was good seeing John, I did a cover for him, but I did in black and white and he changed it to color. It would have been worth more if he'd left it my way but you can never tell anybody anything, I've learned that.

I tried calling again to Billy and John but they wouldn't recognize me it was like I wasn't there. Why won't they let me in. And then I saw Lou. I'm so mad at him. Lou Reed got married and didn't invite me. I mean is it because he thought I'd bring too many people. I don't get it. He could have at least called. I mean he's doing so great. Why doesn't he call me? I saw him at the MTV show and he was one row away and he didn't even say hello. I don't get it. You know I hate Lou I really do. He won't even hire us for his videos. And I was proud of him.

I was so scared today. There was blood leaking through my shirt from those old scars from being shot. And the corset I wear to keep my insides in was hurting. And I did three sets of fifteen pushups and four sets of ten situps. But then my insides hurt and I saw drops of blood on my shirt and I remember the doctors saying I was dead. And then later they had to take blood out of my hand 'cause they ran out of veins but then all this thinking was making me an old grouch and you can't do anything anyway so if they wouldn't let me play with them in my own dream I was just going to have to make another and another and another. Gee wouldn't it be funny if I died in this dream before I could make another one up.

And nobody called.

INTERVIEWS

I WAS backstage at Wembley Stadium. I was there for the Nelson Mandela concert. The weather was typically English. It was hailing and outside 72,000 people were sitting in the cold. I didn't think I would meet Mr. Mandela but I was hoping to at least see him. I had been reading in the press about how the lineup for this Mandela concert was inferior to the previous one—no megastars. That we musicians were politically naive and stupid—didn't we know he was a Communist—he hasn't rejected violence, etc. Plus an interviewer from the BBC with incredibly bad breath had informed me that WEA—my record company—had taken out an ad to retailers saying, "Make Mandela work for you," and what did I have to say about that. Well, they're obviously capitalist dogs, I said, and we should cancel the concert right now, don't you agree. So what if Nelson Mandela went to jail unable to vote and emerged 27 years later still unable to vote—so what that he was being given the opportunity to speak to one billion people this night (except in America—America, where it was deemed too political and people are tired of these benefits anyway).

And no, I didn't get to see Mr. Mandela, not in person anyway. I viewed him on a big video monitor and then on a TV just as you may have. And he was incredible at age 71, at any age, and I hoped I could be that way at that age, and I wondered another thought—how does anyone go to jail for 27 years over an idea. I couldn't comprehend 27 years. Three months, okay. A year. But 27 years. It reminded me of the old Lenny Bruce routine when he's playing a captured soldier and they threaten him—hey, this isn't necessary, here's their time, dates, do you want his home phone number.

This question stayed in my mind because I was leaving the next day to fly to Prague and interview Václav Havel, the new president of Czechoslovakia and a personal hero of mine—a man who like Mandela could have left. They wanted him to leave, he was a successful playwright—why didn't he leave. They'd told him—if you put a wreath on that dead dissident's grave you go to jail. He did it anyway, and went to jail. And now he was president of the country, his cabinet made of various other dissidents, the Communists removed from power, the Czech people rising up to demonstrate 300,000 strong in Wensislav Square for days, finally clashing with the soldiers over the senseless death of a 10-year-old boy. And Václav Havel was no longer in jail but president. A poet, a playwright, a great man.

Before leaving we had had some strange conversations with our Czechoslovakian contacts, exacerbated, no doubt, by the language problem. It was Kafkaesque. Phones dropped off hooks—footsteps clicking down long corridors, it was hard to get clear answers to the most basic requests. The line that made me nervous was when we were told with exasperation—the government will take care of you. I'm from New York. I wouldn't want the government to take care of me. Plus they wanted me to play. At a club. For the local promoter. Visions of various people I knew raced through my mind making me nervous—scalpers, bootlegs, ticket prices. I said no, I didn't want to play for the local promoter. Maybe later when I do a real tour, and no photos or press conference at the airport. After all I said I'm here as a journalist.

PRAGUE is so clean, so elegant, so old. We were in the International Hotel, which at a distance looked to me like a project. Close up it was actually okay, just very boxlike and brown. It had actually been hard to get a room because there were so many journalists and tourists in town. The Pope was coming to Czechoslovakia in two days. We were taken around Prague by Paul, a German photographer, and later by a man who I think became a new old friend, Kočař. Kočař's real name was Kosarek. It's a 400-year-old name and means small carriage. When he grew up his name became Kočař or big carriage. Kočař was a very streetwise person who spoke what he called street English and had resisted all attempts to enroll him in a school to teach him correct grammar. But he spoke just fine. He told us that only a while ago Havel was hiding in his house trying to get the dissidents of Charter 77 together yet again for more protests against the government. And now he was president.

Kočař apologized for the very large, clumsy man following us, another bodyguard. Havel has many enemies. The Communists hate him. And he said, making a gun with his hand and pointing to me, they'd like to hurt his friends. Havel, Kočař said, gets 20 death threats a day. Of course 99 percent of these are not serious. But one might be.

And so we went through Prague waiting for the interview. We saw where the 30-meter bust of Stalin was destroyed. Kočař pointed to the spot with particular revulsion. He'd been 14 in 1968 when the Russian tanks came and had blown up two tanks himself. The Russians are stupid, he said. Their gas tanks are on the rear of the tank quickly available to a hammer and a match and then you run quick. In the demonstration that overturned the Communists he said if you were in the front lines, and he was, the secret was hit and run quick. He had seen an 80-year-old woman beaten by a soldier after she'd told him he was worse than a Nazi. Kočař attacked him and I supposed that was how he lost his front teeth.

We went to the Jewish ghetto and the Jewish cemetery, which was very sad. There was so little land the bodies could not have individual graves—the tombstones were piled atop and next to one another. Isn't that sad, I said. Isn't that beautiful, said our translator Yana, I hope misunderstanding.

We went to the old square. There was a large crowd gathered in front of the astrological clock. On the hour saints popped out of the windows and at the end a brass rooster crowed. We went across the Charles Bridge, named for Charles IV, their greatest king, from the thirteenth century, a king of their people. The bridge had 30 statues of various Catholic icons placed 10 feet from one another on both sides of the bridge. Young kids were playing Beatles' songs and Czech country songs. Prior to Havel no music could be played or sung on the bridge. No young people could gather there. You never knew what they might come up with. We passed a Czech-French film crew. We passed a bust of Kafka on a street but were told not to bother to see his apartment—everything had been ripped out. We ate some dumplings in the oldest restaurant in Prague and then gathered ourselves to go to the castle to meet Václav Havel.

The castle is just that, a large castle in yet another square directly opposite a very beautiful church with a gold-plated clock. We were met outside by Sacha Vandros, the young bespectacled secretary of state. He led us up the red-carpeted stairway to the president's office. We went inside the office and sat at a medium-sized table. The press secretary was to act as our translator. President Havel's English, he said, was not so good. I set up my tape recorder, and suddenly there he was, President Václav Havel.

He's the kind of person you like on sight and things only get better when he talks. He searched for a cigarette and chain-smoked the whole hour. I'd been told he put in 18-hour days, which was a little rough on him since only three weeks ago he'd had a hernia operation. He's one of the nicest men I've ever met. I asked him if it was okay to turn on the tape.

HAVEL: We invite you too for breakfast . . .
REED: No, I mean in the hotel we ordered breakfast and three people came up to give it to us. We thought it was very odd, small tray, three people. So I always thought of Kafka—I think of Kafka when I read you, I er, I'll see if this is working . . .
HAVEL: The State Security was liquidated in our country, but these people work in spite of this fact. I think they are interested more in me than in you, these people.
REED: I don't think so, I don't think so. I don't normally do this.

I've done one other interview in my life, that was two weeks ago. There's a writer I really admire named Hubert Selby, who wrote a book called *Last Exit to Brooklyn,* and a new magazine asked me to interview him. I really wanted to meet him all my life, so I said yes. And it was really wonderful. I got to ask him a lot of questions about writing. So yesterday I found out that that's a great interview. If we had more time I would show it to you. I also have a present for you. Anyway, the magazine rejected the interview.

HAVEL: [*In Czech*] Hang on, I don't understand . . .

INTERPRETER: [*In Czech*] That the magazine rejected it.

HAVEL: [*Laughs*]

INTERPRETER: [*In English*] Was it your idea to do the interview?

REED: It wasn't my idea. It wouldn't occur to me I would be interviewing the president of a country. I was told that I was one of the people who would be acceptable to do an unconventional interview.

HAVEL: Well, I think I have some message work for this magazine, and I would like to tell it to you in this interview, but we must begin immediately because unfortunately I have a lot of work. There are a lot of crises and problems which I have to solve very quickly. And we can begin if you agree. But I would prefer to answer you in Czech and Michael will translate it because he speaks much more better than me.

REED: This is a present for you.

HAVEL: Thank you very much.

REED: That is a CD—

HAVEL: [*In Czech*] Ah yes, this is great. Finally, I'll be able to listen to some music properly.

REED: —of a project called *Songs for 'Drella.* It's about Andy Warhol that I did with John Cale.

HAVEL: I will be very soon in the little village where he was born, Andy Warhol. Meziz Droje. Mezilabolze, very small village in—

[*coffee served*]

REED: No alcohol—

HAVEL: No, no, no. It is forbidden in this castle, only me, I can secretly drink.

HAVEL: [*Through interpreter*] The worst thing about being a president is that I have no time to listen to music. Only the presidential tune . . . And the only time I can listen to music is in my car when I'm going from place to place. Nevertheless I will play the CD as soon as I have the opportunity to. But I equally enjoy good rock music. And sometimes there are even moments when I listen to ugly modern music, commercial music, pop music. For 20 years there was only the most banal pop music in our radio. Now it is already possible to hear on the radio music that previously people could only clandestinely exchange on tapes. And if someone distributed the cassettes for too long, he was usually arrested. Now they are all out of prison and the music is played on the radio.

REED: Is it true that not so long ago, on the Charles Bridge, you couldn't play guitar?

HAVEL: Yes, it is true, the pop musicians there were arrested from time to time. Or at least detained and . . . detained for a while in a police station and then let go. But since we started to talk about music, I'd like to say one thing. That this revolution of ours has, apart from all other faces, also a musical face. Or an artistic face. And it also has a very specific musical background.

At the end of the '60s there was a wave here of rock music. . . . Most of the bands after the Soviet invasion broke up or started playing different music because good rock music was actually banned. There was one band in particular which lasted, which did not rename itself, which did not change. There were several, but this one was the best known. And their style of music was much influenced by the Velvet Underground, whose record I brought back from New York in 1968. It was one of the first records. . . . And this band began to be much persecuted—first they lost their professional status, and then they could only play in private parties. And for a time they also played in the barn of my summer cottage where we had to, in a very complicated way, organize secret concerts. . . . And its name was the Plastic People of the Universe. And there originated around it a whole underground movement in the dark '70s and '80s. Then they were arrested. With several friends we organized a campaign against their arrest, and it was quite hard to convince some very serious gentlemen and academics and Nobel Prize winners to take a stand on behalf of some hairy rock musicians. Nevertheless, we succeeded. And this led to the formation of a community of solidarity of sorts.

Most of these musicians were released and some received light sentences under the pressure of our campaign. And it seemed to us that this community that originated in this way shouldn't just dissolve after this but should go on in some more stable form, and that's how the Charter 77 human rights movement originated.

REED: Really?

HAVEL: The trial with the bands was a special affair. Then it was still possible to enter the court building to be at such a trial. The building was full of people. You could see a university professor in friendly talk with a former member of the Praesidium of the Communist party and with a long-haired rock musician, and all of them surrounded by police.

This was a sign of the things to come, of the special character or nature of the Charter 77, which united many people of different backgrounds and different views in their common resistance to the totalitarian system and in their speaking out against the system. And then some of us got arrested and jailed. But now, members of the Charter 77 are deputies in the parliament, members of the government, or here in the castle.

I myself was one of the first three spokesmen of the Charter 77. By this I mean to say that music, underground music, in particular one record by a band called Velvet Underground, played a rather significant role in the development in our country, and I don't think that many people in the United States have noticed this. So this is one thing I wanted to tell you, and I have another thing to say but maybe in a little while.

But first I should mention that, as is usually the case of rock bands, they undergo changes, they change their names, some of the people leave, etc., etc. Well, the core of this band still exists but it has changed its name and it's now called Midnight—Unots. We had Easter recently, and I turn on the radio in my car while I'm driving to my cottage, and the music they played was Passover music played by this very band, and recorded at my cottage.

REED: Passover music?

HAVEL: Yes, Passover music. The music was recorded about 13 years ago. . . . It was never released before. They just locked themselves in at my cottage for two days and recorded this thing. [*In Czech*] Secretly. It was a very strange experience to suddenly hear this music on Czechoslovak radio.

REED: Joan Baez says hello.

HAVEL: [*In English*] Thank you very much. Please greet her too, and I hope I will see her on the seventh of June when she has to have a concert in Prague. Sixth or seventh, I think. You bring her to Moscow. She will have one concert in Bratislava, I think, and one in Prague.

REED: I admire you so much. In reading *Letters to Olga* . . .

HAVEL: This unread-, unre-

REED: Unreadable.

HAVEL: Unreadable book. It was written in prison, and everything what was understandable, was er, forbidden.

INTERPRETER: Censored.

HAVEL: Censored. Censored, and they learned me to write more and more complicated sentences, and now I don't understand it well.

It is extremely complicated language, but it was the result of pressure of prison censorship, yes, because if they don't understand it, they permit it [*laughs*].

REED: Why was it called the Velvet Revolution?

HAVEL: This name [*In Czech*]. I'll say it in Czech.

HAVEL: [*Through interpreter*] The name was not given to it by us, but by Western journalists. They like simple labels. But the label caught on here. And some people use this word to this day.

Well, it is true that the interesting thing about our revolution was that, except for the first massacre which started it off, there was no blood spilled during the revolution. But it doesn't necessarily mean that it was as velvet as that. Or that we lived in a velvet time. That's just by the way.

I wanted to say another thing for this magazine, if I can volunteer. The whole anti-establishment movement of the '60s had marked significantly my generation and also the generations after that. In 1968, I was in New York for six weeks. I took part in demos and rallies and student protests [*at Columbia University*]. [*In Czech*] As well as that I went to Greenwich Village and the East Village.

REED: Which ones?

HAVEL: They were on strike but they still invited me to give a talk there—I was also at Yale and MIT. And with Milos Forman I participated in be-ins and things like that. We wandered round Greenwich Village, and East Village, and I bought a lot of posters which I still keep. Psychedelic posters which I still have hanging in my cottage.

REED: Did you go to CBGB's?

HAVEL: That was later. Many of the famous musicians like Bob Dylan and Jimi Hendrix were already there, but some only appeared later. [*In Czech*] Recently during the revolution someone stole two of my treasured posters, I don't know why.

REED: So you never saw the Velvet Underground?

HAVEL: Not live, but I bought the record. First edition. At least I think it was the first edition.

REED: Does it have a banana on it?

HAVEL: I haven't seen the record for a long time. I mainly played it at the beginning of the '70s. So I don't remember the banana. But I know it's all black with white letterings [White Light/White Heat *LP*]. And from time to time some rock musicians wanted to steal this record. But I think I still have it. But to go on with what I wanted to say.

The whole spirit of the '60s, the rebellion against the establishment affected significantly the spiritual life of my generation and of the younger people, and in a very strange way, transcended into the present. But we differ from this 20-year-old rebellion in that we made another step further. As small and inconspicuous step as it might be, but it's the knowledge that we can't just tear things down but we have to build in a new way. And many people took political responsibility. And, for example, Michael Kotap, probably the best-known rock musician in this country, is also one of the best-functioning deputies in our Federal Parliament now. He doesn't have much time for composing music. It is a sacrifice of a kind that he has brought to society. But he still managed to write the tune for the castle guards.

And when we were in New York on a state visit two months ago, with Milos Forman, we dropped in to CBGB's one night. And as I learned later, the manager of the place, a man we hadn't really noticed immediately, phoned his friend in Prague that he's got the president of this country in his joint. The people most scared about all this were the 30 people from Secret Service who were supposed to be guarding me. And they were real Rambos. But in the end the Secret Service guys came to like me and they actually gave me a sweater as a present.

And they were moved when I was leaving. But I didn't print things like that.

INTERPRETER: Oh, he says I'm supposed to censor it. I think that's okay.

REED: Do you know that in the United States now they're trying to censor the records? By labeling them?

HAVEL: Well, when we were in the States, they organized a concert in St. John the Divine in New York and there were many famous writers and musicians and other people appearing there, and from them I learned that they also have problems of their own. My heart is always with those who fight for freedom of expression. But it still seems to me that the 200-year-old American democracy is mature enough not to need me as mediator to take messages to Mr. Bush. I think that they can tell him directly.

REED: We try.

HAVEL: They were sort of asking me to plead on their behalf, but I think that would not really be the thing to do. Because in this I would be humiliating them. They are citizens and they can say whatever they want to their elected representatives.

REED: Are you in favor of German reunification?

HAVEL: I think it had to happen sooner or later. And whoever did not think so had no foresight. And if anyone's unprepared for this mentally it's his problem.

INTERPRETER: [To Havel in Czech] I'm having difficulty in translating because I don't get enough time to think.

HAVEL: [To interpreter in Czech] You're the interpreter. Yes, it's a rock magazine. There won't be a scandal, will there?

INTERPRETER: [To Havel in Czech] Not from this, surely?

HAVEL: [Through interpreter] The Berlin Wall was a symbol of the division of Europe. And the fall of this wall was liberation for us all. And it's natural that when the wall falls, the nation reunites itself.

If such a wall went through Prague at the moment it would fall. People would also come together.

REED: You obviously feel and prove that music can change the world.

HAVEL: Not in itself, it's not sufficient in itself. But it can contribute to that significantly in being a part of the awakening of the human spirit. [*Knock at the door. Conversation between Havel and female secretary about things to do and running out of time.*] I think we're running out of time. Is it true or not that you will play at the Gallery tonight?

REED: It was never true that I would play at the Gallery. I brought a guitar with me, though, because I would have played for you, but I wouldn't want to go to a nightclub and play. I would play in private for you as I said, but not in a club. It would make me way too nervous.

HAVEL: I think it would be sort of embarrassing for me if only I could enjoy it and tens of my friends who would like to be there as well could not be there. The bands that I was talking about would be there and people who had been arrested for listening to this kind of music, and friends . . .

REED: Would you be there?

HAVEL: I have a first-night performance of my play tonight. I could be there between 11 and 12, I couldn't make it earlier than 11 and I couldn't stay after 12.

REED: The advantage of being president . . .

HAVEL: There are no advantages at all, but after midnight I still have several speeches to write. And I'm not particularly looking forward to my first night, but the play had been banned before so this is the first time, and the theater struggled for two years to be able to produce it, so this is their first night, so I have to be there. But I could come after . . . But I just have to be there and then thank the actors and company, and shake hands with the actors, and then I could be—

REED: Is this a big club, because if it was President Havel and some friends, I would feel comfortable. But a big club with lots of people—see, I'm a private person.

INTERPRETER: It's not a big club. It's a smallish club, and we were just discussing how many people can—

REED: You see, I'm a very private person, when I came here I didn't want any photographers at the airport, because I don't like my picture taken. I don't like being interviewed—and, er, I like controlled situations—as opposed to just a lot of people. I'm not looking for that. It would be a privilege to play for these people under the right circumstances, but I'm not aware of the circumstances, and it's difficult for me to walk into—

INTERPRETER: I think there would be a couple of hundred people at most. And they would be all friends because it's by invitation.

HAVEL: [*In English*] Mostly musicians, people from Plastic People and from other bands, and Michael Kotap whom I mentioned who is our best deputy in our Assembly and some friends. It would not be public, nobody will know it, and if you don't want to do us, and if you don't want photographers they are not there, and I will not mention to anybody that I will come there, because if I mentioned it anywhere 1000 people would be there together with me, yes.

INTERPRETER: [*In Czech*] They're all friends. There's so many.

HAVEL: [*In English*] We have many friends. But we could arrange that there will be about only 150 friends and we could speak with them and they can play, and if you want you can play for them, et cetera, and I could come there around 11 o'clock and if I would have the opportunity to hear you, I would be very glad. If you prefer only discussion with them and with me, we can discuss it, then I'll leave it.

INTERPRETER: [*In Czech*] Maybe it would help if we could put two or three lads on the door.

HAVEL: [*In English*] It's no problem to arrange that two or three because of my private security could control them.

REED: They'd take care of me.

INTERPRETER: No, just control the entrance so there are only people who are friends get in.

REED: If it's important to the people and it is a request from you, it would be a privilege if the situation is a controlled one, because as I said, I'm very private. So I try always to have control over the situation if I possibly can, so that I can do what I do as well as I can. But if this is something you would like, it would be an honor to do it for you and your people.

HAVEL: I would be very happy if this could happen for me and for people who have been listening to this music for 20 years, so that it became part of their lives, and of course I can guarantee that it will be just those people and no one else. I will be there at 11 plus/minus 10 minutes.

REED: [Laughs]

INTERPRETER: [In Czech] I said plus/minus 10 minutes and he started laughing. [In English] Because I don't know precisely when the play is over. It starts at about 7:30.

REED: Would there be somebody to take me and my wife there?

HAVEL: Sure.

REED: This is a very new situation for me, this city is so beautiful and my admiration for you so enormous, that I would want to do something positive, as long as I knew what it was.

And when it's a mystery to me, I don't know exactly what to do. That's why I said no to almost everything, until I was here and I could speak to someone who could tell me what they thought was right in the situation, which I presume is you.

HAVEL: [In English] We can recommend you right people and we know who we don't recommend you. It's a little bit funny that such things, we do here, in castle, but it is true, and for example, [In Czech] if Lada can be responsible and organize it? [In English] I don't know who all of them tried to contact you and tried to arrange something, but these people are all right who arranged this appointment, we can recommend them. These people from underground, what I explained to you, what was the people and people around them, so-called Czech underground and it's all right.

REED: It was very difficult for me because I never knew whom I was speaking to.

HAVEL: I understand. Of course Sacha my adviser will discuss with you the details about it. I unfortunately have something else to do. Appointments, some minister, somebody—

REED: It was such an honor to meet you, thank you for your time.

KOČAŘ CAME at 10:00 to pick us up and take us to the club which everyone else called the Gallery ("Je Podivna" in Czech). It was dark as we left the ornate buildings and decorative facades of old Prague and headed into new Prague. The Gallery was a medium-sized club with a small stage two feet above the floor where an audience of about 300 now sat. Others milled about talking and sometimes moving to the balcony which stood about 30 feet overhead. The Gallery was also an art gallery, town hall and dissident communication center. We arrived and went down two very wide flights of stairs to the stage area where a band was playing. I commented on how young they looked. Those aren't kids, I was told, the drummer's 42. The band was Pulnoc or Midnight and was made up of members of the Universal Plastic People and the Velvet Underground revival bands. The band consisted of two guitars, electric keyboard, bass, cello and drum and a girl singer. There was an old Fender Twin sitting at the front of the stage just as Kočař had promised. The house system was typical small club, a little boomy in the vocal but otherwise fine.

I suddenly realized the music sounded familiar. They were playing Velvet Underground songs—beautiful, heartfelt, impeccable versions of my songs. I couldn't believe it. This was not something they could have gotten together overnight. The music grew stronger and louder as I listened. "The drummer says he will faint because you are here," said Kočař. "It is their dream come true for you to be in this club to hear them play."

The audience was actually all dissidents. Charter 77 had a membership of 1,800 out of a population of 15,000,000. One after another the songs flew by, each as impassioned as the next, the arrangements, the emphasized lines, the spaces. It was as though I was in a time warp and had returned to hear myself play. To say I was moved would be an understatement. To compose myself I went backstage into what could be called the universal dressing room—small, cold and bare, one bright bulb swinging from the ceiling—and took out my guitar to tune it. My tuner was dead. Its arrows flashed at me with inane irregularity. "I'll get one from the band," said Kočař. And it went dead. Here I am, I thought getting ready to play for these amazing wonderful people, not to mention the president, and I'll be out of tune. Just like the real Velvet Underground. But this band Pulnoc was not a mimic. It was as though they had absorbed the very heart and soul of the VU—all those great ideas and absorbed them into the very marrow of their bones. Steam was rising from me fogging my glasses as I tried tuning by ear. I had sung solo before 72,000 people at Wembley but this was a bit more personal. Then Kočař said, "Havel is here." I looked at my watch. It was 10 after 11.

I went onstage, plugged into the Fender, hit a chord and discovered I was in tune. Well, there's no stopping me now. I did a few songs from my *New York* album realizing they were wordy but aren't all of them. I started to leave the stage when Kočař asked me if the band could join me. They did and we blazed through some old VU numbers. Any song I called they knew. It was as if Moe, John and Sterl were right there behind me and it was a glorious feeling. Soon I had exhausted myself and sweaty but ecstatic I followed Kočař to the balcony and sat down at a table with a beaming Václav Havel.

He'd removed his jacket and loosened his tie. "Did you enjoy yourself?" he asked. "Yes," I said, "I did." "Good," he said. "I'd like you to meet some friends of mine." He then introduced me to an astonishing array of people, all dissidents, all of whom had been jailed. Some had been jailed for playing my music. Many told me of reciting my lyrics for inspiration and comfort when in jail. Some had remembered a line I had written in an essay 15 years ago, "Everybody should die for the music." It was very much a dream for me and well beyond my wildest expectations. When I had gotten out of college and helped form the VU, I had been concerned with, among other things, demonstrating how much more a song could be about than what was currently being written. So the VU albums and my own are implicitly about freedom of expression—freedom to write about what you please in any way you please. And the music had found a home here in Czechoslovakia.

President Havel was having a drink with his friends, something which he does not do in public because he is president. The only time he had for writing was for writing speeches. And the Pope was coming in two days. I thought, imagine a man who writes his own speeches, says his own words. What if George Bush . . . no. Havel said the speeches were easy to write, in fact some resented the fact he said he wrote them so quickly. So now he told them it took longer. He had no time for his own writing, no time to listen to music. No time to have a drink. Foreign policy was not difficult, he said. There are other more unpleasant matters.

And then he was up from the table. "I must go. I have to meet some foreign minister or some such thing. Oh, you must have this," and bending from the waist he handed me a small black book about the size of a diary. "These are your lyrics hand-printed and translated into Czechoslovakian. There were only 200 of them. They were very dangerous to have. People went to jail, and now you have one. Keep your fingers crossed for us."

And he was gone.

The day after next—Havel called it a miracle—the Pope arrived. His and President Havel's speeches were broadcast outdoors through the square. As we left the hotel and took a back road to the airport we still heard their voices. The Pope, we later learned, had warned Havel against the virus, the moral decay of the West. "Maybe he meant you," laughed Kočař. "There," he pointed to an ugly, square, gray building behind wire fencing. "That's where they detained Havel before they sentenced him. You know it's safer to be in an old car than a rich car." He pointed his hand in a gun again. "Better the old car. You know we double the security for the president last night. He must go to club, make things difficult. But to get him would not be so easy. And you had a good time in our country, my friend?"

Yes I did, Kočař. Yes I did. And not a day goes by that I don't think of Václav Havel and the answer he'd given to the question I'd most wanted to ask—"Why did you stay, why didn't you leave? How could you stand the terrible abuse?" And he'd said, "I stayed because I live here. I was only trying to do the right thing. I had not planned for these various things to have happened but I never doubted that we would succeed. All I ever wanted to do was the right thing."

I love Václav Havel. And I'm keeping my fingers crossed. I too want to do the right thing.

I HAD always wanted to meet Hubert Selby. I had thought *Last Exit to Brooklyn* was a great original work, fierce and filled with great rage and tension heralding a Great New Voice—an explosion that leapt off the pages.

HS: I want to put the reader through an emotional experience. My ideal is that the surface of the line would be so intense the reader doesn't even have to read it. [Laughs] I mean it just comes off the page and you absorb it—I mean to use it.
LR: How long did it take to write it?
HS: Six years.
LR: On and off?
HS: No, every night. Every fucking night, man.

Hubert Selby's eyes are blue—a pale blue. There's no redness in them, which is odd since physically he seems to have been through hell. He is missing a lung and some ribs—the result of tuberculosis caught while in the Merchant Marines. He looks like a crouched letter s. He types because longhand is too painful.

HS: It was torture. You know I had to learn to write. For instance, "Tralala"—I think is only twenty pages long or something. I don't know. It's not very long. It took me two and a half years. See, I don't know how to constructively and clearly sit down and think. I have to think out loud even talking with someone or on paper. And most of that time was spent in understanding the stories.

These stories were shown to friends who encouraged him to have them published. Some were, although he's not sure of the names of the magazines.

HS: Finally when I understood what I was supposed to do with the story, then it just [snaps fingers] went like that.

LR: When did that take place?

HS: After two and a half years. [Laughs] And then I—see—I have to understand the story. I think we're all given the story. And it's my responsibility as an artist to understand the story that's been given to me to write—understand the very essence of the story, the psychodynamics of it and from that you create a work of art. So, after two and a half years with "Tralala" I realized that what I had to do in the story was reflect the psychodynamics of an individual, Tralala, through the rhythm and tension of a prose line.

LR: Is this in retrospect?

HS: Well, I didn't figure it out. It just suddenly, after two and a half years, came to me. Ohh! That's what I'm supposed to do. And then it—just went. But, by that time, I'd spent two and a half years going over whatever was in my head, the so-called material, then it just [snaps fingers] went like that.

LR: What do you think of the unique situation in Czechoslavakia?

HS: Why, I'm curious. Why just Czechoslovakia? What's different about that, in so many ways, than the other? I mean, maybe I'm unaware of something. That's why I ask.

LR: Because they made a dissident playwright their president.

HS: Oh, I see. Well, but that's not unusual.

LR: Mmm?

HS: It's not unusual in Eastern Europe. Especially Eastern Europe. In the past, their philosophers, poets, have—and Western Europe, too—have been members of the cabinets, and the parliaments, and leaders. So that's not unusual. I think it's terrific, but it's not unusual. This is the only country where only bad actors have power. You know? You know, not men of imagination. Although the so-called Founding Fathers were all mystic, spiritually oriented people.

LR: Why are you a writer?

HS: Hmm. Buddha said, "Don't ask why." I mean, I don't really know why I'm a writer, but I am. Why I write is I have no choice. I don't really live totally unless I'm writing. And no matter how good I feel before I get in front of a typewriter, I always feel better when I'm . . . I just come alive. I'm more complete. I'm more alive when I'm working. And it's my job.

LR: Do things just come to you?

HS: Well, in a sense, yes, but, of course, that's misleading. I mean, they sometimes may come seemingly from nowhere into my awareness, but most of the time, they're kind of going through a gestation period; I can kind of feel it working its way around, and I kind of hear it, and it comes up and kind of presents itself to my awareness. And I sit down. And there are other times I'm not aware of it until I may suddenly hear a line and write the line, and go on.

LR: How old were you when you wrote it?

HS: When I started. Oh, boy. I guess I was maybe around twenty-eight years old. Let's see. No, I guess I was younger than that. Maybe twenty-six when I started writing. I think. Somewhere around there.

LR: Are you formally religious?

HS: No. Not in the sense of organized religion; church.

LR: Okay. As I recall, various short stories—various chapters in *Exit*—are prefaced by quotes.

HS: Usually, the Old Testament. Yeah.

LR: Is that something that you enjoy reading?

HS: Well, it took me many, many years to learn how to read the Old Testament. I finally found a way, and I enjoy it. And, quite often, I'll do that because it's a book that really contains lots of very simple insights into a very involved situation. You know. Consciousness . . . raised up.

LR: Simple insights?

HS: Yeah. They're usually very clear. Very simple. And about something—

LR: By simple, do you mean universal?

HS: Well, I mean universal, but very simply stated. The truth is always very, very simple when you come across it. But the ramifications of it go on and on. Accept it and assimilate it. And those little lines from the Old Testament usually not only epitomize what's happening in whatever they precede, the story, but it also indicates the answer to the problem that'll be stated in the story.

LR: *Exit* has been made into a movie. Was it difficult to reimmerse yourself in a novel twenty-six years old?

HS: Well, yes and no. I mean, 'cause I didn't actually reimmerse myself in the novel. But I sort of had bits and pieces of it presented to me first in talking about it with the producer and director. So, in going over the outline as originally written by the screenwriter, and then going over the screenplay with them, and watching it being shot, it came in gradual pieces. I mean, it wasn't like jumping into the whole thing. And it was exciting. It was really exciting. I'd lost touch with how much I loved those people.

LR: How much you loved them?

HS: Yeah.

LR: You mean the characters.

HS: Yeah. Yeah, see, I don't think of them as characters. I think of them as people.

LR: Now, I'm sure you must get asked this question all the time. Are those characters made up of various people you know? You know, like "Tralala" isn't really based on a real person; it's based on some characteristics from here, from there, from there?

HS: To a degree. I mean, there was somebody named Tralala. But that's all I know about her. I heard two things one night somewheres, and I remember the night Tralala took her tits out on the bar. And at some other point, somebody said—it could have been months later—they found Tralala naked . . . And that's all I know about Tralala. And the name, a name like Tralala sticks in your mind. And the same thing with "Strike." It's all imagination, but yet it's my experience in life, filtering through my imagination. The only one that approaches being real is Georgie. Georgette. There was a young gay kid named Georgie. So, that part is accurate. The way Georgie is in the book is me. I mean, you know, my imagination . . . whatever.

LR: That's what you think Georgie would think, in the book?

HS: Right.

LR: It's interesting the way you use interior monologues that go from one person's mind to another person's mind to another person's mind. They're never identified. You have to realize who's talking by the way they say it. It doesn't say "thought so and so."

HS: I worked very, very hard to do that. Because I believe that we reflect our inner self in our vocabulary, and in how we utilize that vocabulary, the rhythm of our speech, the juxtaposition of words, of syllables. You see I was raised on the radio—Sam Spade. But the biggest influence that I can think of is the streets. The fucking streets of New York. You don't realize it 'til you go to a place like L.A.; it's so homogenized. You've been in L.A., haven't you?

LR: Oh, yeah.

HS: You know how homogenized the speech is, out there. You can't tell if a guy—if his background is Greek, Italian, Swiss, Irish. Everyone's like Oklahoma. But New York! Oh! The fucking language! The language is just—

LR: Also, it's—

HS: And the . . . just the . . . fucking vitality.

LR: The energy.

HS: Yeah!

LR: I mean, I know when I'm back in New York. There's no missing it—I mean, just looking out the window at the city, then when it lands, the minute you hit the ground, it starts . . .

HS: That's right.

LR: The screaming, the yelling, all of it. It's like I get off on it.

HS: Me, too. I fucking love it. The last time I was here when we shot the film, walking across town in the street, and, you know, there's one of these vendors. You know, a hipster. And he's got some stuff on the street, on a blanket. And there's some dude, bending over, looking at it, and just as I passed [laughs] this guy said, "Hey, I guarantee it."
LR: Oh, I know.
HS: [Laughs]
LR: I'll come back in thirty days.
HS: [Laughs]
LR: It didn't work.
HS: I . . . [laughs]
LR: Yeah. You know, I was on the subway the other day—see, it's an unending source—I was on the subway, the other day, and a guy gets on, and says he's Doctor Double Bubble. Right? And started from there. It was his concept on why you should give him money, and contribute to the homeless. It was a great rap; it deserved some money. I can't imagine that happening other places.
HS: No.
LR: And this is low-level energy. You know. There's the other stuff that obviously gets . . . more intense.
HS: Yeah.
LR: What was your reaction to the idea of making *Exit* a film?
HS: Well, I've always thought it would be a great film, because I write graphically. You know, the way I write is . . . I feel it. And then I hear it. My major conscious influence as a writer is Beethoven. I mean, I visualize it. And then, when I come and write, I try and find the perfect word that will perfectly describe everything I feel, see, and hear. So, it's all a very graphic kind of thing. I mean, I see everything very clearly.
LR: Now, are you a formally educated man?
HS: I left school at fifteen.
LR: So, when you say "search for the perfect word," is—

HS: Or syllable; whatever.

LR: Is the perfect word made available to you from self-education, self-knowledge, or—

HS: We all have the perfection we need.

LR: [Laughs] That's a great answer.

HS: But it's true.

LR: Yeah, of course, it's true.

HS: I just have to move and get out of the way. And let it come up. You know what I mean?

LR: No, I know exactly what you mean.

HS: Yeah. So . . . and, in fact, that's my job. You know, to get my ego out of the way, you know. So I have to find the perfect thing, the perfect note, because, for me, all the typography and everything else are musical notations. So, I have to find the right word, phrase, syllable, punctuation that perfectly describes—and what happens is, if you don't succeed perfectly in doing what I attempt to do, you look like a real fool. I'm still called a barbarian and a [laughs] and an illiterate, in this country.

LR: Is that true?

HS: No, I'm not an illiterate; not at all.

LR: No, no, that—oh, my god, no. That's not what I meant. I meant, is—

HS: Oh.

LR: —is that, I'm sorry.

HS: Oh, no, I wasn't thinking you were insulting me, I thought you were asking me what I feel about myself.

LR: No. No. No, I meant, is it true that you get attacked, still?

HS: Well, they don't bother. Well, for instance, six years ago, I spent the year on welfare. My son and myself. I've applied, over and over, for grants, fellowships . . . but I always get turned down. I got turned down, again, last year, by the NEA.

LR: With the body of work that you have?

HS: They despise me in this country. I'm not saying the readers don't like me. But the established literary community, they ought to know from me. That's one of the reasons I loved going to Europe so much. They respect me over there.

LR: It's interesting that Europe seems to follow people who try to write down their vision of America as realistically as they can—they're taken much more seriously in Europe, and over here, people don't seem to want to hear about it.

HS: Well, a prophet is met with honor, except in his own country. You know, everyone seems to have something to protect. And everyone operates from fear. You know, I don't mean that literally, *everyone*. But most people operate from fear.

LR: Some people operate from anger.

HS: Mmm. Well, fear is the underlying thing. You see, fear needs a form to be effective, and anger is the prevalent form. [Laughs] In one way or another.

LR: Does the fear, anger, apply to yourself and the writing of *Last Exit?*

HS: Oh, absolutely. I mean, if the principle is true in one area, it's true in every area. It must be true for everything and everyone.

LR: That's why I'm asking.

HS: Yeah.

LR: Which form would you say it took?

HS: Well, self-pity. I would say self-pity. You see, for me, the self-pity goes into anger, and then into rage, and so forth. And I thought that was what I was writing from, that very—that anger. And then, since the movie, and seeing what was going on, and seeing my reaction to what was happening to these people, and then reading quotes from me, from 1964. I just read one recently. It just proves to me, again, that, you know, we really don't know ourselves. I thought I was just enraged, and yet, I can see now how the love was so frustrated that I was grappling and groping, and I was crying inside. . . . But I

. . . I couldn't allow myself to get in touch with that. The compassion was overwhelmed by the self-pity in my awareness, and I didn't know that I was crying for me and crying for them. Because I couldn't find a way to just stop and grieve for what had happened to me. So that got misdirected into the fear and self-pity, which just came out of anger and rage. Because I didn't know what to do—I didn't know how to grieve, and say, simply, "You know Cubby? You had a tough life. You got fucked over. So, now, what are we going to do about it?" I couldn't just say that. I've always felt like the battleground of the hounds of heaven and the hounds of hell. Right? You know. It's a scream looking for a mouth—

LR: [Laughs]

HS: You know?

LR: A scream looking for a mouth.

HS: That was me.

THE BELLS

THE BELLS

And the actresses relate
to the actor who comes home late
after the plays have closed down
all the crowds scattered around
through the city lights and the streets
no ticket could beat
that beautiful show of shows
Broadway only knows
The Great White Milky Way
It had something to say
When he fell down on his knees
after soaring through the air
with nothing to hold him there
It was really not cute
to play without a parachute
As he stood upon the ledge
looking out he thought he saw a brook—

and he hollered, "Look! There are the bells!"
and he sang out, "Here come the bells!"
"Here come the bells!"
"Here come the bells!"

/ / *This came to me while we were recording in Germany in the late '70s. I was
experimenting with something called Binaural or 360-degree sound. We had
a beautiful instrumental track with no lyric. On mike I found myself singing
this lyric. Unchanged it remains my favorite to this day.*   / /

DISCOGRAPHY/INDEX